THE

Love Poems

of

ROBERT HERRICK

and

JOHN DONNE

Edited with an Introduction by

LOUIS UNTERMEYER

&NOBLE

B O O K S

N E W   Y O R K

1994 Barnes & Noble Books

ISBN 1-56619-687-6 *hardcover*
ISBN 1-56619-808-9 *paperback*

Printed and bound in the United States of America

MC 9 8 7 6 5 4 3 2
MP 9 8 7 6 5 4 3 2

Contents

THE LOVE POEMS OF ROBERT HERRICK

[v]

ANTHEA

ELECTRA

CORINNA

DIANEME

SAPPHO

SILVIA

BIANCHA

LUCIA

[x]

THE LOVE POEMS OF JOHN DONNE

THE LOVE POEMS

of

ROBERT HERRICK

Introduction

IT MAY SEEM willful or merely whimsical to bring Herrick and Donne together in one volume as exemplars of the poetry of love. Yet their affiliations and dissimilarities, their very contradictions, reveal an extraordinary range of emotions, a complete gamut, with the two poets at either extreme.

Both men were born in London, in the same century, within a few miles and a few years of each other. John Donne was born in 1573, Robert Herrick in 1591. Both men took holy orders, both preached and composed pious epistles, and both continually played variations, "cleanly wanton" or fiercely tortured, on the theme of love. No two men ever wrote more directly and yet more diversely on the same subject.

The contrasts are explicit in every casual set of phrases. Herrick is all delicacy and delight; his Muse is appropriately playful and petulant. Even when Herrick complains of frustration, he does not seem to ache; his greatest protest is little more than a pout. Donne, on the other hand, abjures prettiness and pretense. His images are personal and violently convincing; his conceits range from the agonized to the monstrous. Donne is in complete revolt against the false devices and prim courtliness of the period. He is impatient and brusque, subtle and speculative and shocking in one hurried breath. He plunges the reader into emotion with nervous desperation.

It would be too simple to say that Herrick is all light and Donne is all darkness, yet most of their work falls into those categories. Rarely has the central preoccupation of two contemporary poets evoked greater opposites in style and sensuality. The following pages attempt to match the physical banter of the one with the metaphysical hunger of the other.

II

Robert Herrick, a seventeenth-century vicar, wrote some of the blithest and a few of the naughtiest poems of his age. He was born into a family of jewelers, and it may not be too far-fetched to detect his father's craftsmanship in the poet's finely encrusted, delicately chased and gem-set stanzas.

It was as a goldsmith that Herrick began. At the age of sixteen, he was apprenticed to his uncle, William, and he was particularly skilled in the construction of rings, stick-pins, and brooches. Little is known of his early manhood, but he seems to have been well educated; his father was prosperous, and young Herrick attended Cambridge for about two years. He graduated from Trinity Hall in 1616, the year of Shakespeare's death. He seems to have studied for the law, but there is no record of his having practiced the profession. In London, he became part of a group that gathered about Ben Jonson, who "adopted" Herrick as his literary stepchild. Rumor had him occasionally roistering at the taverns frequented by the more literate young blades, and it was as "a son of Ben" that Herrick began to write verses that were both witty and wanton.

In 1629, when Herrick was thirty-eight, he received a small ecclesiastical living; he was presented with the vicarage of Dean Prior in Devonshire. There he passed the next eighteen years of his life. His occupancy of a pulpit in the peaceful countryside should have been pleasant. But his life in Devonshire was far from idyllic. Herrick was restless in the country. Although his verse is full of blossoms, birds, and bowers, he longed for London; no rural scenery delighted him as much as the streets of tawdry Cheapside. He

[4]

regarded his bucolic surroundings as an enforced retirement, almost a prison. He made a few friends but, on the whole, he resented the country folk who, not unnaturally, resented him. He characterized his neighbors as:

> A people currish; churlish as the seas;
> And rude, almost, as rudest savages.

He missed his beloved London with a sense of bitter isolation. He continued to complain:

> More discontents I never had,
> Since I was born, than here;
> Where I have been, and still am, sad
> In this dull Devonshire.

Nevertheless, it was not the town Muse but the country Muse who inspired him. It was not only a fantastic imagination but an accurate observation which, in the midst of querulous moods, helped him to create his carefree poems. He was conscious of the paradox. He confessed that he never intended so many "ennobled numbers" as in the place where he "loathed so much" to be. Almost against his will, he relished the half-Puritan, half-pagan customs of the countryside: the rough rustic games; the undemanding company of his maid, Prue; his teasing little spaniel, his pet lamb, and his pet pig which he trained to drink beer from a tankard. He sometimes lost patience with his dull-witted parishioners —it is reported that he once threw the manuscript of his sermon at the sleepy members of his congregation, with a curse at their inattention. But he was inevitably drawn into the circle of their lives. He may have objected to the dullness of his surroundings, but he drew his substance—and his best poems—from the simple earth.

The environment of Dean Prior directed and almost dictated Herrick's ambling lines. The bucolic wakes and gay wassails, the spring daffodils and autumn harvests, the merrymakers jostling in farm wagons and shouting around Maypoles furnished him with all the drama he needed. They became his plot and his properties; he acknowledged it in the couplets appropriately entitled "The Argument of His Book:"

> I sing of brooks, of blossoms, birds, and bowers:
> Of April, May, of June, and July flowers.
> I sing of Maypoles, hock-carts, wassails, wakes,
> Of bridegrooms, brides, and of their bridal-cakes.
> I write of youth, of love, and have access
> By these, to sing of cleanly wantonness.
> I sing of dews, of rains, and piece by piece
> Of balm, of oil, of spice, and amber-greece.
> I sing of times trans-shifting; and I write
> How roses first came red, and lilies white.
> I write of groves, of twilights, and I sing
> The court of Mab, and of the fairy king.
> I write of Hell. I sing (and ever shall)
> Of Heaven, and hope to have it after all.

III

In his fifty-seventh year, Herrick lost his livelihood. He had supported the King during the Civil War and was forced to give up his position during the Commonwealth. He was by no means unhappy to return to London; it is apparent that he considered himself lucky to escape the monotonous "confines of the drooping west." His haven was the metropolis. "I fly," he wrote, "to thee, blest place of my nativity." He said it before; he reaffirmed it now:

> London my home is: though by hard fate sent
> Into a long and dreary banishment.

Hoping to re-establish himself among his fellow poets, Herrick went up to London in 1648 and published a collection of his poems. It was entitled *Hesperides*, a volume which contained almost everything he had written. It was not much of a success. Jonson had died, and his coterie had been dissipated. The critics of the period regarded Herrick's naïve enthusiasms with condescension and belittled his pastoral simplicities. One contemporary wrote that "Prue was but indifferently qualified to be a tenth Muse." The next generation forgot him. It was not until 1796—more than a century after Herrick's death—that he was "discovered" by John Nichols and reread with surprise.

After the Restoration, Herrick regained the pulpit which he had given up to John Syms. He was seventy-one when, in 1662, he succeeded his successor and once more resigned himself to the quiet of Devonshire. He lived there another twelve years, and died at Totnes in 1674, in his eighty-fourth year.

IV

Herrick charms us today not merely by his prettiness but by a kind of mocking purity. His verse is licentious but seldom lewd; his tone may be carnal but it is never gross. Although Herrick has been compared to Horace and Propertius, he is actually more akin to Catullus. He is a refinement of all his models. His exquisite mistresses are too numerous for truth, too coyly perfect for reality. But, if they are unreal, they are as haunting and as tantalizing as a recurrent dream.

It is apparent that there was a wide split between Herrick's poetic (public) sensuality and his private practice. Even when he prides himself on being wanton, he insists so repetitively that the reader is rarely deceived. Time and again Herrick abandons the libertine pose. Fearful that the reader may take him literally, he disclaims practically everything. In a couplet entitled "Poets" he reassures us definitely:

> Wantons we are; and though our words be such,
> Our lives do differ from our lines by much.

Herrick emphasizes the sentiment with an almost pathetic caution. He repeats it significantly in what he well may have wanted to serve as his "Last Words":

> To his book's end this last line he'd have placed:
> Jocund his Muse was; but his life was chaste.

This is the uncomplicated key to the paradox, the union of naughtiness and niceties, of wishful sensuousness and practical common sense. It is by no means a titanic paradox, and the verse which reflects it is not earth-shaking. Essentially, Herrick's poetry is a triumph of tiny significances. Here are details almost too small to notice but which, somehow, remain large in the reader's memory. The lines are bound together with tissues and textures, with azure robes and careless shoestrings, with a tempestuous petticoat, a bit of filmy lawn thrown about the shoulders in "a fine distraction," an "erring lace" and the "brave vibration" of a silken dress, sweetly disordered ribbons and coy rosebuds. Never has a writer done so much with such trivial material. It may be said that Herrick trifled his way from light verse into lasting poetry.

The author of some thirteen hundred poems, Herrick never attempted the long line. His poems are compact and short; many of them are thumbnail miniatures. He never tried to tear a passion to tatters; he was content to be a poet of pleasure, a nimble epicurean. His attitude to life was simple: beauty was evanescent, love was capricious, time was swift. Such easy platitudes served instead of a philosophy; Herrick's fine-spun lines could not have borne anything weightier.

Yet, even when his work is most frail, it is superbly finished, serene and spontaneous. The keynote is a lyric dexterity, an airy playfulness. Herrick's song never has the soaring rapture of Shelley's skylark, nor has it the pure ecstasy of Keats's nightingale. His is a graceful but homely strain, a domestic sort of singing. It has the lilt of a small bird, the house-wren, full of the pert and happy repetitions of a songster that is no less ingratiating and fascinating for being so agelessly familiar.

Louis Untermeyer

Note: The antique punctuation and the archaic (and often inconsistent) spellings in the poetry of both Herrick and Donne have been corrected and modernized. The poems themselves have been rearranged and newly grouped by the editor.

CREDO

To the Virgins, to Make Much of Time

GATHER ye rosebuds while ye may,
   Old time is still a flying,
And this same flower that smiles today,
   Tomorrow will be dying.

The glorious lamp of Heaven, the sun,
   The higher he's a getting,
The sooner will his race be run,
   And nearer he's to setting.

That age is best which is the first,
   When youth and blood are warmer;
But being spent, the worse, and worst
   Times still succeed the former.

Then be not coy, but use your time,
   And while ye may, go marry;
For having lost but once your prime,
   You may forever tarry.

Delight in Disorder

A SWEET disorder in the dress
Kindles in clothes a wantonness.
A lawn about the shoulders thrown
Into a fine distractión;
An erring lace, which here and there
Enthralls the crimson stomacher;
A cuff neglectful, and thereby
Ribbons to flow confusedly;
A winning wave (deserving note)
In the tempestuous petticoat;
A careless shoestring, in whose tie
I see a wild civility —
Do more bewitch me than when art
Is too precise in every part.

Julia

--- ✳ ---

Upon Julia's Clothes

WHENAS in silks my Julia goes,
Then, then, methinks, how sweetly flows
That liquefaction of her clothes.

Next, when I cast mine eyes and see
That brave vibration, each way free,
O how that glittering taketh me!

Upon Julia's Fall

JULIA was careless, and withal
She rather took, then got a fall.
The wanton ambler chanced to see
Part of her legs sincerity;
And ravished thus, it came to pass
The nag, like to the prophet's ass,
Began to speak, and would have been
A telling what rare sights he'd seen,
And had told all, but did refrain,
Because his tongue was tied again.

Upon Julia's Voice

SO smooth, so sweet, so silvery is thy voice,
As, could they hear, the damned would make no noise,
But listen to thee walking in thy chamber,
Melting melodious words to lutes of amber.

Upon Julia's Petticoat

THY azure robe I did behold,
As airy as the leaves of gold;
Which erring here, and wandering there,
Pleased with transgression everywhere.
Sometimes 't would pant, and sigh, and heave,
As if to stir it scarce had leave:
But having got it, thereupon,
'T would make a brave expansión;
And pounced with stars, it showed to me
Like a celestial canopy.
Sometimes 't would blaze, and then abate,
Like to a flame grown moderate:
Sometimes away 't would wildly fling,
Then to thy thighs so closely cling,
That some conceit did melt me down,
As lovers fall into a swoon;
And all confused, I there did lie
Drowned in delights, but could not die.
That leading cloud I followed still,
Hoping t' have seen of it my fill;
But ah! I could not: should it move
To life eternal, I could love.

Upon Julia's Ribbon

AS shows the air, when with a rainbow graced;
So smiles the ribbon round my Julia's waist;
Or like—nay 't *is* the zonulet of love,
Wherein all pleasures of the world are wove.

Julia Disdainful: or, The Frozen Zone

WHITHER? Say, whither shall I fly,
To slack these flames wherein I fry?
To the treasures, shall I go,
Of the rain, frost, hail, and snow?
Shall I search the underground,
Where all damps, and mists are found?
Shall I seek, for speedy ease,
All the floods, and frozen seas?
Or descend into the deep,
Where eternal cold does keep?
These may cool; but there's a zone
Colder yet than any one:
That's my Julia's breast; where dwells
Such destructive icicles;
As that the congealation will
Me sooner starve, than those can kill.

Upon Julia's Unlacing Herself

TELL, if thou canst, and truly, whence doth come
This camphire, storax, spikenard, galbanum;
These musks, these ambers, and those other smells,
Sweet as the vestry of the oracles.
I'll tell thee. While my Julia did unlace
Her silken body, but a breathing space,
The passive air such odor then assumed,
As when to Jove great Juno goes perfumed.
Whose pure immortal body doth transmit
A scent that fills both heaven and earth with it.

Upon the Nipples of Julia's Breast

HAVE ye beheld, with much delight,
A red rose peeping through a white?
Or else a cherry, double graced,
Within a lily's center placed?
Or ever marked the pretty beam
A strawberry shows, half drowned in cream?
Or seen rich rubies blushing through
A pure smooth pearl, and orient too?
So like to this, nay all the rest,
Is each neat niplet of her breast.

Upon Julia's Hair Filled With Dew

DEW sat on Julia's hair,
And spangled too
Like leaves that laden are
With trembling dew;
Or glittered to my sight,
As when the beams
Have their reflected light
Danced by the streams.

Upon the Roses in Julia's Bosom: 1

THRICE happy roses, so much graced to have
Within the bosom of my love your grave,
Die when ye will, your sepulcher is known;
Your grave her bosom is, the lawn the stone.

Upon the Roses in Julia's Bosom: 2

ROSES, you can never die,
Since the place wherein ye lie,
Heat and moisture mixed are so,
As to make ye ever grow.

The Rosary

ONE asked me where the roses grow;
   I bade him not go seek,
But forthwith bade my Julia show
   A bud in either cheek.

Upon Julia's Hair, Bundled Up
in a Golden Net

TELL me, what needs those rich deceits,
These golden toils and trammel-nets,[1]
To take thine hairs, when they are known
Already tame, and all thine own?
'T is I am wild, and more than hairs
Deserves these meshes and those snares.
Set free thy tresses; let them flow
As airs do breathe or winds do blow;
And let such curious networks be
Less set for them than spread for me.

[1] Trammel-nets: delicate braids folding the hair in a sort of snood.

Upon Julia's Recovery

DROOP, droop no more, or hang the head
Ye roses almost witheréd;
Now strength, and newer purple get,
Each here declining violet.
O primroses! Let this day be
A resurrection unto ye;
And to all flowers allied in blood,
Or sworn to that sweet sisterhood:
For health on Julia's cheek hath shed
Claret, and cream commingléd.
And those her lips do now appear
As beams of coral, but more clear.

Upon Julia's Singing

WHEN I thy singing next shall hear,
I'll wish I might turn all to ear,
To drink in notes, and numbers; such
As blessed souls can't hear too much.
Then melted down, there let me lie
Entranced, and lost confusedly:
And by thy music stricken mute,
Die, and be turned into a lute.

Upon His Julia

WILL ye hear, what I can say
Briefly of my Julia?
Black and rolling is her eye,
Double-chinned and forehead high:
Lips she has, all ruby red,
Cheeks like cream enclareted:
And a nose that is the grace
And proscenium of her face.
So that we may guess by these,
The other parts will richly please.

Upon Julia's Breasts

DISPLAY thy breasts, my Julia, there let me
Behold that circummortal purity:
Between whose glories, there my lips I'll lay,
Ravished, in that fair *Via Lactea*.

Upon Julia's Washing Herself
in the River

HOW fierce was I, when I did see
My Julia wash herself in thee!
So lilies thorough crystal look,
So purest pebbles in the brook,
As in the river Julia did,
Half with a lawn of water hid.
Into thy streams myself I threw,
And struggling there I kissed thee too;
And more had done, it is confessed,
Had not the waves forbade the rest.

Art Above Nature: To Julia

WHEN I behold a forest spread
With silken trees upon thy head,
And when I see that other dress
Of flowers set in comeliness;
When I behold another grace
In the ascent of curious lace,
Which like a pinacle doth show
The top, and the top-gallant too;
Then, when I see thy tresses bound
Into an oval, square, or round,
And knit in knots far more than I
Can tell by tongue, or true-love tie;
Next, when those lawny films I see
Play with a wild civility,
And all those airy silks to flow,
Alluring me, and tempting so:
I must confess, mine eye and heart
Dotes less on nature than on art.

Upon Her Feet

HER pretty feet
Like snails did creep
   A little out, and then,
As if they started at Bo-peep,
   Did soon draw in again.

Upon Roses

UNDER a lawn than skies more clear,
Some ruffled roses nestling were;
And snugging there, they seemed to lie
As in a flowery nunnery.
They blushed, and looked more fresh than flowers
Quickened of late by pearly showers;
And all, because they were possessed
But of the heat of Julia's breast,
Which as a warm and moistened spring,
Gave them their ever flourishing.

The Parliament of Roses: To Julia

I DREAMT the roses one time went
To meet and sit in Parliament.
The place for these, and for the rest
Of flowers, was thy spotless breast,
Over the which a state was drawn
Of tiffany, or cobweb lawn.
Then, in that parley, all those powers
Voted the rose the Queen of flowers;
But so, as that herself should be
The Maid of Honor unto thee.

The Weeping Cherry

I SAW a Cherry weep, and why?
  Why wept it? but for shame,
Because my Julia's lip was by,
  And did out-red the same.
But pretty fondling, let not fall
  A tear at all for that:
Which Rubies, Corals, Scarlets, all
  For tincture, wonder at.

Cherry-Ripe

CHERRY—Ripe! ripe! ripe! I cry,
Full and fair ones; come and buy:
If so be, you ask me where
They do grow? I answer, "There,
Where my Julia's lips do smile;
There's the land, or cherry isle,
Whose plantations fully show
All the year, where Cherries grow!"

To Daisies, Not to Shut So Soon

SHUT not so soon; the dull-eyed night
   Has not as yet begun
To make a seizure on the light,
   Or to seal up the sun.

No marigolds yet closéd are,
   No shadows great appear;
Nor doth the early shepherds' star
   Shine like a spangle here.

Stay but till my Julia close
   Her life-begetting eye;
And let the whole world then dispose
   Itself to live or die.

The Night-Piece: To Julia

HER eyes the glow-worm lend thee,
The shooting stars attend thee;
    And the elves also,
    Whose little eyes glow
Like the sparks of fire, befriend thee.

No Will-o'-the-Wisp mislight thee,
Nor snake or slow-worm bite thee;
    But on, on thy way,
    Not making a stay,
Since ghost there's none to affright thee.

Let not the dark thee cumber
What though the moon does slumber?
    The stars of the night,
    Will lend thee their light,
Like tapers clear without number.

Then Julia let me woo thee,
Thus, thus to come unto me;
    And when I shall meet
    Thy silvery feet,
My soul I'll pour into thee.

The Bracelet to Julia

WHY I tie about thy wrist,
Julia, this my silken twist,
For what other reason is't,
But to show thee how, in part,
Thou my pretty captive art?
But thy bondslave is my heart.
'T is but silk that bindeth thee;
Snap the thread, and thou art free;
But 't is otherwise with me:
I am bound, and fast bound so,
That from thee I cannot go;
If I could, I would not so.

The Pomander Bracelet

TO me my Julia lately sent
A bracelet richly redolent:
The beads I kissed, but most loved her
That did perfume the pomander.[1]

Her Bed

SEE'ST thou that cloud as silver clear,
Plump, soft, and swelling everywhere?
'T is Julia's bed, and she sleeps there.

[1] Pomander: Balls or beads of aromatic substances, often carried instead of perfume.

A Ring Presented to Julia

JULIA, I bring
To thee this ring,
Made for thy finger fit;
To show by this,
That our love is,
Or should be, like to it.

Close though it be,
The joint is free:
So when love's yoke is on,
It must not gall,
Or fret at all
With hard oppressión.

But it must play
Still either way;
And be, too, such a yoke,
As not too wide,
To over-slide,
Or be so strait to choke.

So we, who bear
This beam, must rear
Ourselves to such a height,
As that the stay
Of either may
Create the burden light.

And as this round
Is nowhere found

To flaw, or else to sever,
So let our love
As endless prove,
And pure as gold forever.

The Rock of Rubies and the Quarry of Pearls

SOME asked me where the Rubies grew?
  And nothing I did say:
But with my finger pointed to
  The lips of Julia.
Some asked how Pearls did grow, and where?
  Then spoke I to my girl,
To part her lips, and showed them there
  The quarrylets of Pearl.

The Captived Bee:
or, the Little Filcher

AS Julia once a slumbering lay,
It chanced a bee did fly that way,
After a dew, or dew-like shower,
To tipple freely in a flower.
For some rich flower he took the lip
Of Julia, and began to sip;
But when he felt he sucked from thence
Honey, and in the quintessence,
He drank so much he scarce could stir.
So Julia took the pilferer,
And thus surprised, as filchers use,
He thus began himself t' excuse: —
Sweet lady-flower, I never brought
Hither the least one thieving thought;
But taking those rare lips of yours
For some fresh, fragrant, luscious flowers,
I thought I might there take a taste,
Where so much syrup ran to waste.
Besides, know this, I never sting
The flower that gives me nourishing,
But with a kiss, or thanks, do pay
For honey that I bear away.
This said, he laid his little scrip
Of honey 'fore her ladyship;
And told her, as some tears did fall,
That that he took, and that was all.
At which she smiled, and bade him go
And take his bag, but thus much know:
When next he came a pilfering so,

He should from her full lips derive
Honey enough to fill his hive.

The Silken Snake

FOR sport my Julia threw a lace
Of silk and silver at my face;
Watchet [1] the silk was; and did make
A show as if it had been a snake:
The suddenness did me affright;
But though it scared, it did not bite.

Upon Her Blush

WHEN Julia blushes, she does show
Cheeks like to roses when they blow.

[1] Watchet: a bluish-green color.

To the Fever, Not to Trouble Julia

THOU hast dared too far; but, Fury, now forbear
To give the least disturbance to her hair:

But less presume to lay a plait upon
Her skins most smooth, and clear expansión.

'T is like a lawny firmament as yet
Quite dispossessed of either fray or fret.

Come thou not near that film so finely spread,
Where no one piece is yet unlevelléd.

This if thou dost, woe to thee, Fury, woe,
I'll send such frost, such hail, such sleet, and snow,

Such flesh-quakes, palsies, and such fears as shall
Dead thee to th' most, if not destroy thee all.

And thou a thousand thousand times shalt be
More shaken thyself than she is scorched by thee.

The Maiden-Blush

SO look the mornings when the sun
Paints them with fresh vermilion:
So cherries blush, and Katherine pears,
And apricots, in youthful years:
So corals look more lovely red,
And rubies lately polishéd:
So purest diaper [1] doth shine,
Stained by the beams of claret wine:
As Julia looks when she doth dress
Her either cheek with bashfullness.

To Julia in the Temple

BESIDES us two, i' th' temple here's not one
To make up now a congregatión.
Let's to the altar of perfumes then go,
And say short prayers; and when we have done so,
Then we shall see how, in a little space,
Saints will come in to fill each pew and place.

[1] Diaper: fine linen towel or napkin.

To Julia in Her Dawn or Daybreak

BY the next kindling of the day,
    My Julia, thou shalt see,
Ere Ave Mary thou canst say
    I'll come and visit thee.

Yet ere thou counsel'st with thy glass,
    Appear thou to mine eyes
As smooth and naked as she that was
    The prime of Paradise.

If blush thou must, then blush thou through
    A lawn, that thou may'st look
As purest pearls or pebbles do,
    When peeping through a brook;

As lilies shrined in crystal, so
    Do thou to me appear;
Or damask roses when they grow
    To sweet acquaintance there.

Julia's Anger: Tears Are Tongues

WHEN Julia chid, I stood as mute the while
As is the fish, or tongueless crocodile.
Air coined to words, my Julia could not hear,
But she could see each eye to stamp a tear:
By which mine angry mistress might descry,
Tears are the noble language of the eye:
And when true love of words is destitute,
The eyes by tears speak, while the tongue is mute.

To Julia: 1

PERMIT me, Julia, now to go away,
Or by thy love decree me here to stay.
If thou wilt say that I shall live with thee,
Here shall my endless tabernacle be:
If not, as banished I will live alone
There where no language ever yet was known.

To Julia: 2

FIRST, for your shape, the curious cannot show
Any one part that's dissonant in you:
And 'gainst your chaste behavior there's no plea,
Since you are known to be Penelope.
Thus fair and clean you are, although there be
A mighty strife 'twixt form and chastity.

To Julia: 3

HELP me, Julia, for to pray,
Matins sing, or matins say:
This I know, the Fiend will fly
Far away, if thou beest by.
Bring the holy water hither;
Let us wash, and pray together:
When our beads are thus united,
Then the Foe will fly affrighted.

His Covenant: or, Protestation to Julia

WHY dost thou wound and break my heart,
As if we should forever part?
Hast thou not heard an oath from me,
After a day, or two, or three,
I would come back and live with thee?
Take, if thou dost distrust that vow,
This second protestation now.
Upon thy cheek that spangled tear
Which sits as dew of roses there,
That tear shall scarce be dried before
I'll kiss the threshold of thy door.
Then weep not, sweet, but this much know:
I'm half returned before I go.

The Rainbow: or, Curious Covenant

MINE eyes, like clouds, were drizzling rain,
And as they thus did entertain
The gentle beams from Julia's sight
To mine eyes levelled opposite:
O thing admired! There did appear
A curious rainbow smiling there;
Which was the covenant, that she
No more would drown mine eyes, or me.

The Bride-Cake

THIS day my Julia thou must make
For Mistress Bride, the wedding cake:
Knead but the dough, and it will be
To paste of almonds turned by thee:
Or kiss it thou, but once, or twice,
And for the Bride-Cake there'll be spice.

How His Soul Came Ensnared

MY soul would one day go and seek
For roses, and in Julia's cheek,
A richness of those sweets she found,
As in another Rosamond.
But gathering roses as she was,
Not knowing what would come to pass
It chanced a ringlet of her hair,
Caught my poor soul, as in a snare:
Which ever since has been in thrall.
Yet freedom, she enjoys withal!

His Last Request to Julia

I HAVE been wanton, and too bold I fear,
To chafe o'er much the virgins' cheek or ear.
Beg for my pardon, Julia; he doth win
Grace with the gods who's sorry for his sin.
That done, my Julia, dearest Julia, come,
And go with me to choose my burial room.
My fates are ended; when thy Herrick dies,
Clasp thou his book, then close thou up his eyes.

To Julia: Last Words

JULIA, when thy Herrick dies,
Close thou up thy poet's eyes;
And his last breath, let it be
Taken in by none but thee.

Anthea

———————— ✳ ————————

To Anthea, Who May Command Him Anything

BID me to live, and I will live
    Thy protestant to be:
Or bid me love, and I will give
    A loving heart to thee.

A heart as soft, a heart as kind,
    A heart as sound and free
As in the whole world thou canst find,
    That heart I'll give to thee.

Bid that heart stay, and it will stay,
    To honor thy decree:
Or bid it languish quite away,
    And 't shall do so for thee.

Bid me to weep, and I will weep,
    While I have eyes to see:
And having none, yet I will keep
    A heart to weep for thee.

Bid me despair, and I'll despair,
    Under that cypress tree:
Or bid me die, and I will dare
    E'en death, to die for thee.

Thou art my life, my love, my heart,
    The very eyes of me,
And hast command of every part
    To live and die for thee.

To Anthea: 1

NOW is the time, when all the lights wax dim;
And thou, Anthea, must withdraw from him
Who was thy servant. Dearest, bury me
Under that Holy-oak, or Gospel-tree:
Where (though thou see'st not) thou may'st think upon
Me, when thou yearly go'st Procession:
Or for mine honor, lay me in that tomb
In which thy sacred relics shall have room:
For my embalming, Sweetest, there will be
No spices wanting, when I'm laid by thee.

To Anthea: 2

AH, my Anthea! Must my heart still break?
Love makes me write what shame forbids to speak.
Give me a kiss, and to that kiss a score;
Then to that twenty, add an hundred more;
A thousand to that hundred; so kiss on,
To make that thousand up a million;
Treble that million, and when that is done,
Let's kiss afresh, as when we first begun.
But yet, though love likes well such scenes as these,
There is an act that will more fully please:
Kissing and glancing, soothing, all make way
But to the acting of this private play:
Name it I would; but being blushing red,
The rest I'll speak, when we meet both in bed.

To Anthea: 3

SICK is Anthea, sickly is the spring,
The primrose sick, and sickly every thing.
The while my dear Anthea does but droop,
The tulips, lilies, daffodils do stoop;
But when again she's got her healthful hour,
Each bending then will rise a proper flower.

To Anthea: 4

ANTHEA, I am going hence
With some small stock of innocence,
But yet those blesséd gates I see
Withstanding entrance unto me.
To pray for me do thou begin,
The porter then will let me in.

To Anthea: 5

LET'S call for Hymen if agreed thou art;
Delays in love but crucify the heart.
Love's thorny tapers yet neglected lie:
Speak thou the word, they'll kindle by and by.
The nimble hours woo us on to wed,
And Genius waits to have us both to bed.
Behold, for us the naked Graces stay
With mounds of roses for to strew the way:
Besides, the most religious prophet stands
Ready to join as well our hearts as hands.
Juno yet smiles; but if she chance to chide,
Ill luck 't will bode to th' bridegroom and the bride.
Tell me, Anthea, dost thou fondly dread
The loss of that we call a maidenhead?
Come, I'll instruct thee: Know, the vestal fire
Is not by marriage quenched, but flames the higher.

The Shoe-Tying

ANTHEA bade me tie her shoe;
I did, and kissed the instep too,
And would have kissed unto her knee,
Had not her blush rebukéd me.

To Anthea Lying in Bed

SO looks Anthea, when in bed she lies,
O'ercome, or half betrayed, by tiffanies,[1]
Like to a twilight, or that simpering dawn,
That roses show when misted o'er with lawn.
Twilight is yet, till that her lawns give way;
Which done, that dawn turns then to perfect day.

Love Perfumes All Parts

IF I kiss Anthea's breast,
There I smell the Phoenix' nest:
If her lip, the most sincere
Attar of incense, I smell there.
Hands, and thighs, and legs, are all
Richly aromatical.
Goddess Isis can't transfer
Musks and ambers more from her,
Nor can Juno sweeter be,
When she lies with Jove, than she.

[1] Tiffany: an almost transparent muslin or silk gauze.

The Wake

COME, Anthea, let us two
Go to feast, as others do.
Tarts and custards, creams and cakes
Are the junkets still at wakes:
Unto which the tribes resort,
Where the business is the sport.
Morris-dancers thou shalt see,
Marian too in pageantry,
And a mimic to devise
Many grinning properties.
Players there will be, and those
Base in action, as in clothes:
Yet with strutting they will please
The incurious villages.
Near the dying of the day,
There will be a cudgel-play,
Where a coxcomb will be broke,
Ere a good word can be spoke.
But the anger ends all here,
Drenched in ale, or drowned in beer.
Happy rustics! best content
With the cheapest merriment:
And possess no other fear,
Than to want the wake next year.

Electra

To Electra: 1

I DARE not ask a kiss;
    I dare not beg a smile;
Lest having that or this,
    I might grow proud the while.

No, no, the utmost share
    Of my desire shall be,
Only to kiss that air
    That lately kisséd thee.

To Electra: 2

SHALL I go to Love and tell
Thou art all turned icicle?
Shall I say her altars be
Disadorned and scorned by thee?
O beware! in time submit;
Love has yet no wrathful fit:
If her patience turns to ire,
Love is then consuming fire.

To Electra: 3

I'LL come to thee in all those shapes
As Jove did when he made his rapes;
Only, I'll not appear to thee
As he did once to Semele.
Thunder and lightning I'll lay by,
To talk with thee familiarly:
Which done, then quickly we'll undress
To one and th' others nakedness;
And ravished, plunge into the bed,
Bodies and souls commingléd,
And kissing, so as none may hear,
We'll weary all the fables there.

To Electra: 4

MORE white than whitest lilies far,
Or snow, or whitest swans you are:
More white than are the whitest creams,
Or moonlight tinseling the streams:
More white than pearls, or Juno's thigh,
Or Pelop's arm of ivory.
True, I confess, such whites as these
May me delight, not fully please,
Till, like Ixion's cloud, you be
White, warm, and soft to lie with me.

To Electra: 5

'T IS evening, my sweet,
    And dark; let us meet;
Long time we've here been a toying:
    And never, as yet,
    That season could get,
Wherein to have had an enjoying.

    For pity or shame,
    Then let not love's flame
Be ever and ever a spending;
    Since now to the port
    The path is but short,
And yet our way has no ending.

    Time flies away fast,
    Our hours do waste,
The while we never remember,
    How soon our life here
    Grows old with the year,
That dies with the next December.

To Electra: 6

WHEN out of bed my love doth spring,
'T is but as day a kindling:
But when she's up and fully dressed,
'T is then broad day throughout the east.

To Electra: Love Looks for Love

LOVE love begets; then never be
Unsoft to him who's smooth to thee:
Tigers and bears, I've heard some say,
For proffered love will love repay.
None are so harsh, but, if they find   '
Softness in others, will be kind.
Affection will affection move:
Then you must like, because I love.

Upon Her Weeping

SHE wept upon her cheeks, and weeping so,
She seemed to quench love's fires that there did glow.

Upon Her Voice

LET but thy voice engender with the string,
And angels will be born while thou dost sing.

To Electra: The Vision

I DREAMED we both were in a bed
Of roses, almost smotheréd:
The warmth and sweetness had me there
Made lovingly familiar,
But that I heard thy sweet breath say,
Faults done by night will blush by day.
I kissed thee panting, and I call
Night to the record, that was all.
But ah! if empty dreams so please,
Love, give me more such nights as these.

Corinna

--- ✳ ---

Corinna's Going A Maying

GET up, get up for shame, the blooming morn
Upon her wings presents the god unshorn.
 See how Aurora throws her fair
 Fresh-quilted colors through the air!
 Get up, sweet slug-a-bed, and see
 The dew-bespangling herb and tree.
Each flower has wept, and bow'd toward the east,
Above an hour since; yet you not dressed,
 Nay! not so much as out of bed?
 When all the birds have matins said,
 And sung their thankful hymns, 't is sin,
 Nay, profanation to keep in,
When as a thousand virgins on this day,
Spring, sooner than the lark, to fetch in May.

Rise, and put on your foliage, and be seen
To come forth, like the springtime, fresh and green
 And sweet as Flora. Take no care
 For jewels for your gown or hair.
 Fear not; the leaves will strew
 Gems in abundance upon you.
Besides, the childhood of the day has kept,
Against you come, some orient pearls unwept:
 Come, and receive them while the light
 Hangs on the dew-locks of the night,

And Titan on the eastern hill
Retires himself, or else stands still
Till you come forth. Wash, dress, be brief in praying:
Few beads are best, when once we go a Maying.

Come, my Corinna, come; and coming, mark
How each field turns a street, each street a park
    Made green, and trimmed with trees: see how
    Devotion gives each house a bough
    Or branch: each porch, each door, ere this,
    An ark, a tabernacle is,
Made up of white-thorn neatly interwove;
As if here were those cooler shades of love.
    Can such delights be in the street
    And open fields, and we not see 't?
    Come, we'll abroad; and let's obey
    The proclamation made for May,
And sin no more, as we have done, by staying;
But, my Corinna, come, let's go a Maying.

There's not a budding boy, or girl, this day,
But is got up, and gone to bring in May.
    A deal of youth, ere this, is come
    Back, and with white-thorn laden home.
    Some have dispatched their cakes and cream,
    Before that we have left to dream:
And some have wept, and wooed, and plighted troth,
And chose their priest, ere we can cast off sloth.
    Many a green-gown has been given;
    Many a kiss, both odd and even;
    Many a glance too has been sent
    From out the eye, love's firmament;
Many a jest told of the keys betraying
This night, and locks picked, yet we're not a Maying.

Come, let us go, while we are in our prime,
And take the harmless folly of the time.
    We shall grow old apace, and die
    Before we know our liberty.
    Our life is short, and our days run
    As fast away as does the sun;
And as a vapor, or a drop of rain,
Once lost, can ne'er be found again,
    So when or you or I are made
    A fable, song, or fleeting shade,
    All love, all liking, all delight,
    Lies drowned with us in endless night.
Then while time serves, and we are but decaying;
Come, my Corinna, come, let's go a Maying.

The Eye: To Corinna

MAKE me a heaven, and make me there
Many a less and greater sphere;
Make me the straight and oblique lines,
The motions, lations,[1] and the signs;
Make me a chariot and a sun,
And let them through a zodiac run.
Next, place me zones and tropics there,
With all the seasons of the year;
Make me a sunset, and a night,
And then present the morning's light
Clothed in her chamlets [2] of delight.
To these, make clouds to pour down rain,
With weather foul, then fair again.
And when, wise artist, that thou hast
With all that can be this heaven graced,
Ah! what is then this curious sky.
But only my Corinna's eye?

[1] Lations: movements of bodies from one place to another.
[2] Chamlet: a soft and costly fabric, usually made of finely mixed materials.

The Changes: To Corinna

BE not proud, but now incline
Your soft ear to discipline.
You have changes in your life,
Sometimes peace, and sometimes strife;
You have ebbs of face and flows,
As your health or comes, or goes:
You have hopes, and doubts, and fears,
Numberless as are your hairs:
You have pulses that do beat
High, and passions less of heat:
You are young, but must be old,
And to these, ye must be told,
Time, ere long, will come and plow
Loathéd furrows in your brow:
And the dimness of your eye
Will no other thing imply,
But you must die
As well as I.

Dianeme

———— ✳ ————

To Dianeme: 1

SWEET, be not proud of those two eyes,
Which starlike sparkle in their skies:
Nor be you proud, that you can see
All hearts your captives; yours, yet free:
Be you not proud of that rich hair,
Which wantons with the lovesick air:
When as that ruby, which you wear,
Sunk from the tip of your soft ear,
Will last to be a precious stone,
When all your world of beauty's gone.

To Dianeme: 2

DEAR, though to part it be a hell,
Yet, Dianeme, now farewell:
Thy frown, last night, did bid me go,
But whither, only grief does know.
I do beseech thee, ere we part,
(If merciful as fair thou art;
Or else desir'st that maids should tell
Thy pity by loves-chronicle)
O Dianeme, rather kill
Me, than to make me languish still!
'Tis cruelty in thee to th' height,
Thus, thus to wound, not kill outright;
Yet there's a way found, if thou please,
By sudden death to give me ease;
And thus devised: —do thou but this,
Bequeath to me one parting kiss:
So sup'rabundant joy shall be
The executioner of me.

To Dianeme: 3

SHOW me thy feet, show me thy legs, thy thighs,
Show me those fleshy principalities;
Show me that hill where smiling love doth sit,
Having a living fountain under it;
Show me thy waist: then let me there withal,
By the ascension of thy lawn, see all.

To Dianeme: 4

GIVE me one kiss
    And no more;
If so be this
    Makes you poor,
To enrich you,
    I'll restore
For that one two
    Thousand score.

To Dianeme: 5

I COULD but see thee yesterday
    Stung by a fretful bee,
And I the javelin sucked away,
    And healed the wound in thee.

A thousand thorns and briars and stings
    I have in my poor breast,
Yet ne'er can see that salve which brings
    My passions any rest.

As Love shall help me, I admire
    How thou canst sit and smile
To see me bleed, and not desire
    To stanch the blood the while.

If thou, composed of gentle mould,
    Art so unkind to me,
What dismal stories will be told
    Of those that cruel be?

Sappho

———— * ————

To Sappho

LET us now take time and play,
Love and live here while we may;
Drink rich wine, and make good cheer
While we have our being here;
For, once dead and laid i' th' grave,
No return from thence we have.

The Sadness of Things
for Sappho's Sickness

LILIES will languish; violets look ill;
Sickly the primrose; pale the daffodil:
That gallant tulip will hang down his head,
Like to a virgin newly ravishéd.

Pansies will weep, and marigolds will wither;
And keep a fast and funeral together,
If Sappho droop; daisies will open never,
But bid good-night, and close their lids forever.

How Roses Came Red

ROSES at first were white,
  Till they could not agree,
Whether my Sappho's breast,
  Or they more white should be.

But being vanquished quite,
  A blush their cheeks bespread;
Since which (believe the rest!)
  The roses first came red.

The Apron of Flowers

TO gather flowers Sappho went,
  And homeward she did bring,
Within her lawny continent,
  The treasure of the spring.

She smiling blushed, and blushing smiled,
  And sweetly blushing thus,
She looked as she'd been got with child
  By young Favonius.

Her apron gave, as she did pass,
  An odor more divine,
More pleasing, too, than ever was
  The lap of Proserpine.

Upon Sappho, Sweetly Playing
and Sweetly Singing

WHEN thou do'st play, and sweetly sing,
Whether it be the voice or string,
Or both of them, that do agree
Thus to entrance and ravish me:
This, this I know, I'm oft struck mute;
And die away upon thy lute.

The Headache

MY head doth ache,
O Sappho! take
　　Thy fillet,
And bind the pain;
Or bring some bane
　　To kill it.

But less that part
Than my poor heart,
　　Now is sick:
One kiss from thee
Will counsel be,
　　And physic.

The Tear Sent to Her From Stanes

GLIDE, gentle streams, and bear
Along with you my tear
  To that coy girl,
  Who smiles, yet slays
  Me with delays,
And strings my tears as pearl.

See! see, she's yonder set,
Making a carcanet [1]
  Of maiden-flowers!
  There, there present
  This orient,
And pendant pearl of ours.

Then say, I've sent one more
Gem to enrich her store;
  And that is all
  Which I can send,
  Or vainly spend,
For tears no more will fall.

Nor will I seek supply
Of them, the springs once dry;
  But I'll devise,
  (Among the rest)
  A way that's best
How I may save mine eyes.

Yet say, should she condemn
Me to surrender them;

[1] Carcanet: a necklace, usually of gold or jewels.

Then say, my part
Must be to weep
Out them, to keep
A poor, yet loving heart.

Say too, she would have this.
She shall: Then my hope is,
   That when I'm poor,
   And nothing have
   To send, or save,
I'm sure she'll ask no more.

Silvia

───── * ─────

To Silvia, To Wed

LET us (though late) at last, my Silvia, wed,
And loving lie in one devoted bed.
Thy watch may stand, my minutes fly post haste;
No sound calls back the year that once is past.
Then, sweetest Silvia, let's no longer stay;
True love, we know, precipitates delay,
Away with doubts, all scruples hence remove;
No man at one time can be wise and love.

A Song Upon Silvia

FROM me my Silvia ran away,
   And running there withal;
A primrose bank did cross her way,
   And gave my love a fall.

But trust me now I dare not say,
   What I by chance did see;
But such the drapery did betray
   That fully ravished me.

To Silvia

PARDON my trespass, Silvia, I confess,
My kiss outwent the bounds of shamefastness:
None is discreet at all times; no, not Jove
Himself, at one time, can be wise and Love.

Upon Silvia, A Mistress

WHEN some shall say, "Fair once my Silvia was,"
Thou wilt complain, "False now's thy looking-glass,
Which renders that quite tarnished which was green,
And priceless now what peerless once had been.
Upon thy form more wrinkles yet will fall;
And coming down shall make no noise at all."

Biancha

—————————— * ——————————

To Biancha, To Bless Him

WOULD I woo thee, and would I win,
Would I well my work begin?
Would I evermore be crowned
With the end that I propound?
Would I frustrate or prevent
All aspects malevolent;
Thwart all wizards, and with these
Dead all black contingencies;
Place my words, and all works else,
In most happy parallels?
All will prosper, if so be
I be kissed or blessed by thee.

Being Once Blind, His Request
to Biancha

WHEN age or chance has made me blind,
So that the path I cannot find;
And when my falls and stumblings are
More than the stones i' th' street by far;
Go thou afore, and I shall well
Follow thy perfumes by the smell:
Or be my guide, and I shall be
Led by some light that flows from thee.
Thus held or led by thee, I shall
In ways confused nor slip or fall.

Kissing Usury

BIANCHA, let
Me pay the debt
I owe thee for a kiss
Thou lend'st to me;
And I to thee
Will render ten for this:

If thou wilt say,
Ten will not pay
For that so rich a one;
I'll clear the sum,
If it will come
Unto a millión.

By this I guess,
Of happiness
Who has a little measure,
He must of right,
To th' utmost mite,
Make payment for his pleasure.

Lucia

———— ✳ ————

Upon Lucia Dabbled in the Dew

M Y Lucia in the dew did go,
And prettily bedabbled so,
Her clothes held up, she showed withal
Her decent legs, clean, long and small.
I followed after to descry
Part of the naked sincerity;
But still the envious veil between
Denied the mask I would have seen.

To Carnations: For Lucia

S T A Y while ye will, or go;
   And leave no scent behind ye:
Yet trust me, I shall know
   The place, where I may find ye.

Within my Lucia's cheek
   (Whose livery ye wear)
Play ye at Hide-or-Seek,
   I'm sure to find ye there.

The Vine

I DREAMED this mortal part of mine
Was metamorphosed to a vine,
Which, crawling one and every way,
Enthralled my dainty Lucia.
Methought, her long small legs and thighs
I with my tendrils did surprise;
Her belly, buttocks, and her waist
By my soft nervelets were embraced:
About her head I writhing hung,
And with rich clusters hid among
The leaves, her temples I behung:
So that my Lucia seemed to me
Young Bacchus ravished by his tree.
My curls about her neck did crawl,
And arms and hands they did enthrall,
So that she could not freely stir,
All parts there made one prisoner.
But when I crept with leaves to hide
Those parts which maids keep unespied,
Such fleeting pleasures there I took
That with the fancy I awoke;
And found, ah me! this flesh of mine
More like a stock than like a vine.

Perenna

———— ✱ ————

To Perenna

WHEN I thy parts run o'er, I can't espy
In any one the least indecency,
But every line and limb diffuséd thence,
A fair and unfamiliar excellence:
So that the more I look, the more I prove
There's still more cause why I the more should love.

To the Western Wind

SWEET western wind, whose luck it is,
    Made rival with the air,
To give Perenna's lip a kiss,
    And fan her wanton hair—

Bring me but one, I'll promise thee,
    Instead of common showers,
Thy wings shall be embalmed by me,
    And all beset with flowers.

Perilla

———————— * ————————

His Protestation to Perilla

NOONDAY and midnight shall at once be seen:
Trees, at one time, shall be both sere and green:
Fire and water shall together lie
In one self sweet conspiring sympathy:
Summer and winter shall at one time show
Ripe ears of corn, and up to th' ears in snow,
Seas shall be sandless, fields devoid of grass,
Shapeless the world as when all Chaos was,
Before, my dear Perilla, I will be
False to my vow or fall away from thee.

Oenone

———————— ✳ ————————

To Oenone

WHAT conscience, say, is it in thee
   When I a heart had one,
To take away that heart from me,
   And to retain thy own?

For shame or pity now incline
   To play a loving part;
Either to send me kindly thine,
   Or give me back my heart.

Covet not both; but if thou dost
   Resolve to part with neither;
Why! yet to show that thou art just,
   Take me and mine together.

Myrrha

———— ✳ ————

To Myrrha, Hard-Hearted

FOLD now thine arms, and hang the head,
Like to a lily witheréd:
Next, look thou like a sickly moon,
Or like Jocasta in a swoon.
Then weep, and sigh, and softly go,
Like to a widow drowned in woe:
Or like a virgin full of ruth,
For the lost sweetheart of her youth:
And all because, fair maid, thou art
Insensible of all my smart;
And of those evil days that be
Now posting on to punish thee.
The gods are easy, and condemn
All such as are not soft like them.

Phillis

―――――― ✱ ――――――

To Phillis, to Love and Live With Him

LIVE, live with me, and thou shalt see
The pleasures I'll prepare for thee.
What sweets the country can afford
Shall bless thy bed, and bless thy board.
The soft sweet moss shall be thy bed,
With crawling woodbine overspread;
By which the silver-shedding streams
Shall gently melt thee into dreams.
Thy clothing, next, shall be a gown
Made of the fleece's purest down.
The tongues of kids shall be thy meat;
Their milk thy drink; and thou shalt eat
The paste of filberts for thy bread,
With cream of cowslips butteréd.
Thy feasting-tables shall be hills
With daisies spread, and daffodils;
Where thou shalt sit, and red-breast by,
For meat, shall give thee melody.
I'll give thee chains and carcanets
Of primroses and violets.
A bag and bottle thou shalt have;
That richly wrought, and this as brave
So that as either shall express
The wearer's no mean shepherdess.
At shearing-times and yearly wakes,

When Themilis his pastime makes,
There thou shalt be, and be the wit,
Nay more, the feast and grace of it.
On holy-days, when virgins meet
To dance the hays with nimble feet,
Thou shalt come forth, and then appear
The queen of roses for that year.
And having danced, 'bove all the best
Carry the garland from the rest.
In wicker baskets maids shall bring
To thee, my dearest shepherdling,
The blushing apple, bashful pear,
And shame-faced plum, all simpering there.
Walk in the groves, and thou shalt find
The name of Phillis in the rind
Of every straight and smooth-skin tree;
Where kissing that, I'll twice kiss thee.
To thee a sheep-hook I will send
Bepranked with ribbons to this end—
This, this alluring hook might be
Less for to catch a sheep than me.
Thou shalt have possets, wassails fine,
Not made of ale, but spicéd wine;
To make thy maids and self free mirth,
All sitting near the glittering hearth.
Thou shalt have ribbons, roses, rings,
Gloves, garters, stockings, shoes, and strings
Of winning colors, that shall move
Others to lust but me to love.
These, nay, and more, thine own shall be,
If thou wilt love, and live with me.

Irene

———— ✱ ————

Upon Irene

ANGRY if Irene be
But a minute's life with me,
Such a fire I espy
Walking in and out her eye,
As at once I freeze and fry.

Flora

---- ✳ ----

To Violets

WELCOME, maids of honor!
    You do bring
    In the Spring,
And wait upon her.

She has virgins many
    Fresh and fair;
    Yet you are
More sweet than any.

Y' are the maiden posies,
    And so graced,
    To be placed
'Fore damask roses.

Yet though thus respected,
    By and by
    Ye do lie,
Poor girls! neglected.

To the Rose

GO, happy rose, and, interwove
With other flowers, bind my love.
   Tell her, too, she must not be
   Longer flowing, longer free,
   That so oft has fettered me.

Say, if she's fretful, I have bands
Of pearl and gold to bind her hands:
   Tell her if she struggle still,
   I have myrtle rods at will
   For to tame, though not to kill.

Take thou my blessing thus, and go,
And tell her this: but do not so,
   Lest a handsome anger fly,
   Like a lightning, from her eye,
   And burn thee up as well as I.

To Blossoms

FAIR pledges of a fruitful tree,
    Why do ye fall so fast?
    Your date is not so past,
But you may stay yet here a while,
    To blush and gently smile,
      And go at last.

What, were ye born to be
    An hour or half's delight,
    And so to bid goodnight?
'T was pity nature brought ye forth
    Merely to show your worth,
      And lose you quite.

But you are lovely leaves, where we
    May read how soon things have
    Their end, though ne'er so brave;
And after they have shown their pride,
    Like you, a while, they glide
      Into the grave.

The Primrose

ASK me why I send you here
This sweet infanta of the year?
    Ask me why I send to you
This primrose, thus bepearled with dew?
    I will whisper to your ears,
The sweets of love are mixed with tears.

    Ask me why this flower doth show
So yellow-green, and sickly too?
    Ask me why the stalk is weak
And bending, yet it doth not break?
    I will answer, these discover
What fainting hopes are in a lover.

To Primroses Filled
With Morning Dew

WHY do ye weep, sweet babes? can tears
        Speak grief in you,
        Who were but born
     Just as the modest morn
     Teemed her refreshing dew?
Alas, you have not known that shower
        That mars a flower;
        Nor felt th' unkind
     Breath of a blasting wind;
     Nor are ye worn with years,
        Or warped, as we,
     Who think it strange to see
Such pretty flowers, like to orphans young
To speak by tears before ye have a tongue.
Speak, whimp'ring younglings, and make known
        The reason why
        Ye droop and weep.
     Is it for want of sleep,
     Or childish lullaby?
   Or that ye have not seen as yet
        The violet?
        Or brought a kiss
     From that sweetheart to this?—
     No, no, this sorrow shown
        By your tears shed,
     Would have this lecture read:
That things of greatest, so of meanest worth,
Conceived with grief are and with tears brought forth.

To the Willow Tree

THOU art to all lost love the best,
   The only true plant found,
Wherewith young men and maids distressed,
   And left of love, are crowned.

When once the lover's rose is dead,
   Or laid aside forlorn,
Then willow-garlands 'bout the head,
   Bedewed with tears, are worn.

When with neglect, the lover's bane,
   Poor maids rewarded be
For their love lost, their only gain
   Is but a wreath from thee.

And underneath thy cooling shade,
   When weary of the light,
The love-spent youth and love-sick maid
   Come to weep out the night.

To Daffodils

FAIR Daffodils, we weep to see
  You haste away so soon:
As yet the early-rising sun
  Has not attained his noon.
      Stay, stay,
    Until the hasting day
       Has run
    But to the even song;
And, having prayed together, we
    Will go with you along,

We have short time to stay as you,
  We have as short a spring;
As quick a growth to meet decay,
  As you, or any thing.
      We die,
    As your hours do, and dry
      Away
    Like to the summer's rain,
  Or as the pearls of morning's dew
    Ne'er to be found again.

To Sycamores

I'M sick of Love; O let me lie
Under your shades, to sleep or die!
Either is welcome; so I have
Or here my bed, or here my grave.
Why do you sigh, and sob, and keep
Time with the tears, that I do weep?
Say, have ye sense, or do you prove
What crucifixions are in love?
I know ye do; and that's the why
You sigh for Love, as well as I.

To Springs and Fountains

I HEARD ye could cool heat, and came
With hope you would allay the same.
Thrice I have washed, but feel no cold,
Nor find that true, which was foretold.
Methinks like mine, your pulses beat;
And labor with unequal heat.
Cure, cure yourselves, for I descry
Ye boil with love, as well as I!

The Lily in a Crystal

YOU have beheld a smiling rose
    When virgins hands have drawn
    O'er it a cobweb-lawn:
And here, you see, this lily shows,
    Tombed in a crystal stone,
More fair in this transparent case
    Than when it grew alone,
    And had but single grace.

You see how cream but naked is,
    Nor dances in the eye
    Without a strawberry,
Or some fine tincture like to this,
    Which draws the sight thereto
More by that wantoning with it,
    Than when the paler hue
    No mixture did admit.

You see how amber through the streams
    More gently strokes the sight,
    With some concealed delight,
Then when he darts his radiant beams
    Into the boundless air;
Where either too much light his worth
    Doth all at once impair,
    Or set it little forth.

Put purple grapes, or cherries, in-
    To glass, and they will send
    More beauty to commend

Them from that clean and subtle skin,
    Than if they naked stood,
And had no other pride at all
    But their own flesh and blood,
    And tinctures natural.

Thus lily, rose, grape, cherry, cream,
    And strawberry do stir
    More love when they transfer
A weak, a soft, a broken beam,
    Than if they should discover
At full their proper excellence,
    Without some screen cast over,
To juggle with the sense.

Thus let this crystalled lily be
    A rule, how far to teach
    Your nakedness must reach:
And that no further than we see
    Those glaring colors laid
By Art's wise hand, but to this end,
    They should obey a shade,
    Lest they too far extend.

So though y' are white as swan or snow,
    And have the power to move
    A world of men to love,
Yet, when your lawns and silks shall flow,
    And that white cloud divide
Into a doubtful twilight, then,
    Then will your hidden pride
    Raise greater fires in men.

The Bleeding Hand:
or, the Sprig of Eglantine

FROM this bleeding hand of mine,
Take this sprig of eglantine.
Which (though sweet unto your smell)
Yet the fretful briar will tell,
He who plucks the sweets shall prove
Many thorns to be in love.

How Lilies Came White

WHITE though ye be, yet, lilies, know,
From the first ye were not so;
    But I'll tell ye
    What befell ye:
Cupid and his mother lay
In a cloud; while both did play,
He with his pretty finger pressed
The ruby niplet of her breast;
Out of the which, the cream of light,
    Like to a dew,
    Fell down on you,
    And made ye white.

Why Flowers Change Color

THESE fresh beauties, we can prove,
Once were virgins sick of love,
Turned to flowers. Still in some
Colors go, and colors come.

The Willow Garland

A WILLOW garland thou did'st send
    Perfumed (last day) to me:
Which did but only this portend,
    I was forsook by thee.

Since so it is, I'll tell thee what,
    Tomorrow thou shalt see
Me wear the willow; after that,
    To die upon the tree.

As beasts unto the altars go
    With garlands dressed, so I
Will with my willow-wreath also,
    Come forth and sweetly die.

The Shower of Blossoms

LOVE in a shower of blossoms came
Down, and half drowned me with the same:
The blooms that fell were white and red;
But with such sweets commingléd,
As whether (this I cannot tell)
My sight was pleased more, or my smell:
But true it was, as I rolled there,
Without a thought of hurt, or fear;
Love turned himself into a bee,
And with his javelin wounded me:
From which mishap this use I make,
Where most sweets are, there lies a snake.
Kisses and favors are sweet things;
But those have thorns, and these have stings.

Varia

————————— ✳ —————————

The Mad Maid's Song

GOOD morrow to the day so fair;
  Good morning, sir, to you;
Good morrow to mine own torn hair
  Bedabbled with the dew.

Good morning to this primrose too,
  Good morrow to each maid
That will with flowers the tomb bestrew,
  Wherein my love is laid.

Ah! woe is me, woe, woe is me,
  Alack and welladay!
For pity, sir, find out that bee
  Which bore my love away.

I'll seek him in your bonnet brave,
  I'll seek him in your eyes;
Nay, now I think t' have made his grave
  I' th' bed of strawberries.

I'll seek him there; I know, ere this,
  The cold, cold earth doth shake him:
But I will go, or send a kiss
  By you, sir, to awake him.

Pray hurt him not; though he be dead,
    He knows well who do love him,
And who with green-turfs rear his head,
    And who do rudely move him.

He's soft and tender! pray take heed!
    With bands of cowslips bind him,
And bring him home. But 'tis decreed,
    That I shall never find him.

Upon the Loss of His Mistresses

I HAVE lost, and lately, these
Many dainty mistresses:
Stately Julia, prime of all;
Sappho next, a principal;
Smooth Anthea, for a skin
White, and heaven-like crystalline;
Sweet Electra, and the choice
Myrrha, for the lute and voice;
Next, Corinna, for her wit,
And the graceful use of it,
With Perilla. All are gone;
Only Herrick's left alone,
For to number sorrow by
Their departures hence, and die.

To His Mistresses

HELP me! help me! now I call
To my pretty witchcrafts all:
Old I am, and cannot do
That I was accustomed to.
Bring your magics, spells, and charms,
To enflesh my thighs and arms.
Is there no way to beget
In my limbs their former heat?
Æson had, as poets fain,
Baths that made him young again:
Find that medicine, if you can,
For your dry, decrepit man;
Who would fain his strength renew,
Were it but to pleasure you.

To His Mistress' Objecting to Him Neither Toying nor Talking

YOU say I love not, 'cause I do not play
Still with your curls, and kiss the time away.
You blame me, too, because I can't devise
Some sport to please those babies in your eyes.
By Love's religion, I must here confess it,
The most I love when I the least express it.
Small griefs find tongues: full casks are ever found
To give, if any, yet but little sound.

To His Lovely Mistresses

ONE night i' th' year, my dearest beauties come
And bring those dew drink-offerings to my tomb.
When thence ye see my reverend ghost to rise,
And there to lick th' effuséd sacrifice,
Though paleness be the livery that I wear,
Look ye not wan or colorless for fear.
Trust me, I will not hurt ye, or once show
The least grim look, or cast a frown on you:
Nor shall the tapers, when I'm there, burn blue.
This I may do, perhaps, as I glide by,
Cast on my girls a glance and loving eye:
Or fold mine arms and sigh, because I've lost,
The world so soon, and in it you, the most.
Then these, no fears more on your fancies fall,
Though then I smile, and speak no words at all.

What Kind of Mistress He Would Have

BE the mistress of my choice
Clean in manners, clear in voice;
Be she witty, more than wise;
Pure enough, though not precise:
Be she showing in her dress,
Like a civil wilderness;
That the curious may detect
Order in a sweet neglect:
Be she rolling in her eye,
Tempting all the passers-by;
And each ringlet of her hair
An enchantment, or a snare
For to catch the lookers on,
But herself held fast by none.
Let her Lucrece all day be,
Thaïs in the night, to me.
Be she such, as neither will
Famish me, nor over-fill.

A Meditation for His Mistress

YOU are a tulip seen today
But, dearest, of so short a stay,
That where you grew, scarce man can say.

You are a lovely July-flower,
Yet one rude wind, or ruffling shower,
Will force you hence, and in an hour.

You are a sparkling rose i' th' bud,
Yet lost, ere that chaste flesh and blood
Can show where you or grew, or stood.

You are a full-spread fair-set vine,
And can with tendrils love intwine,
Yet dried, ere you distill your wine.

You are like balm enclosèd well
In amber, or some crystal shell,
Yet lost ere you transfuse your smell.

You are a dainty violet,
Yet withered, ere you can be set
Within the virgin's coronet.

You are the queen all flowers among,
But die you must, fair maid, ere long,
As he, the maker of this song.

His Misery in a Mistress

WATER, water I espy:
Come, and cool ye; all who fry
In your loves; but none as I.

Though a thousand showers be
Still a falling, yet I see
Not one drop to light on me.

Happy you, who can have seas
For to quench ye, or some ease
From your kinder mistresses.

I have one and she alone,
Of a thousand thousand known,
Dead to all compassión.

Such an one as will repeat
Both the cause, and make the heat
More by provocation great.

Gentle friends, though I despair
Of my cure, do you beware
Of those girls which cruel are.

To His Mistress

CHOOSE me your valentine;
  Next, let us marry:
Love to the death will pine
  If we long tarry.

Promise, and keep your vows,
  Or vow ye never:
Love's doctrine disallows
  Troth-breakers ever.

You have broke promise twice,
  Dear, to undo me;
If you prove faithless thrice,
  None then will woo you.

To Music, to Becalm His Fever

CHARM me asleep, and melt me so,
  With thy delicious numbers,
That being ravished, hence I go
  Away in easy slumbers.
  Ease my sick head,
  And make my bed,
Thou power that canst sever
  From me this ill,
  And quickly still,
  Though thou not kill,
    My fever.

Thou sweetly canst convert the same
From a consuming fire,
Into a gentle-licking flame,
And make it thus expire.
Then make me weep
My pains asleep,
And give me such reposes,
That I, poor I,
May think thereby,
I live and die
'Mongst roses.

Fall on me like a silent dew,
Or like those maiden showers,
Which, by the peep of day, do strew
A baptism o'er the flowers.
Melt, melt my pains,
With thy soft strains,
That having ease me given,
With full delight,
I leave this light,
And take my flight
For heaven.

To the Maids, to Walk Abroad

COME sit we under yonder tree,
Where merry as the maids we'll be;
And as on primroses we sit,
We'll venture (if we can) at wit:

If not, at draw-gloves we will play,
So spend some minutes of the day:
Or else spin out the thread of sands,
Playing at questions and commands,
Or tell what strange tricks love can do,
By quickly making one of two.
Thus we will sit and talk; but tell
No cruel truths of Philomel,
Or Phillis, whom hard fate forced on,
To kill herself for Demophon.
But fables we'll relate: how Jove
Put on all shapes to get a love;
And now a satyr, then a swan;
A bull but then, and now a man.
Next we will act how young men woo,
And sigh, and kiss, as lovers do;
And talk of brides, and who shall make
That wedding-smock, this bridal-cake;
That dress, this sprig, that leaf, this vine,
That smooth and silken columbine.
This done, we'll draw lots who shall buy
And gild the bays and rosemary;
What posies for our wedding rings,
What gloves we'll give, and ribbonings;
And smiling at ourselves, decree
Who then the joining priest shall be;
What short sweet prayers shall be said,
And how the posset shall be made
With cream of lilies, (not of kine),
And maiden's blush, for spicéd wine.
Thus having talked, we'll next commend
A kiss to each, and so we'll end.

The Vision: 1

SITTING alone, as one forsook,
Close by a silver-shedding brook,
With hands held up to love, I wept,
And after sorrows spent, I slept:
Then in a vision I did see
A glorious form appear to me:
A virgin's face she had; her dress
Was like a sprightly Spartaness.
A silver bow, with green silk strung,
Down from her comely shoulders hung;
And as she stood, the wanton air
Dandled the ringlets of her hair.
Her legs were such Diana shows,
When tucked up she a hunting goes,
With buskins shortened to descry
The happy dawning of her thigh:
Which when I saw, I made access
To kiss that tempting nakedness;
But she forbade me, with a wand
Of myrtle she had in her hand,
And chiding me, said, "Hence, remove.
Herrick, thou art too coarse to love."

The Vision: 2

METHOUGHT I saw (as I did dream in bed)
A crawling vine about Anacreon's head:
Flushed was his face; his hairs with oil did shine;
And as he spake, his mouth ran o'er with wine.
Tippled he was; and tippling lisped withal;
And lisping reeled, and reeling like to fall.
A young enchantress close by him did stand
Tapping his plump thighs with a myrtle wand:
She smiled; he kissed; and kissing, culled her, too;
And being cup-shot, more he could not do.
For which (methought) in pretty anger she
Snatched off his crown, and gave the wreath to me:
Since when (methinks) my brains about do swim,
And I am wild and wanton like to him.

Upon a Black Twist Rounding the Arm of the Countess of Carlile

I SAW about her spotless wrist,
Of blackest silk a curious twist;
Which, circumvolving gently, there
Enthralled her arm as prisoner.
Dark was the jail, but as if light
Had met t' engender with the night;
Or so as darkness made a stay
To show at once both night and day.
I fancy more; but if there be
Such freedom in captivity,
I beg of Love that ever I
May in like chains of darkness lie.

No Luck in Love

I DO love I know not what;
Sometimes this, and sometimes that;
All conditions I aim at.

But, as luckless, I have yet
Many shrewd disasters met
To gain her whom I would get.

Therefore now I'll love no more
As I've doted heretofore:
He who must be, shall be poor.

In the Dark None Dainty

NIGHT hides our thefts; all faults then pardoned be;
All are alike fair, when no spots we see.
Laïs and Lucrece in the night time are
Pleasing alike, alike both singular.
Joan and my lady have at that time one,
One and the selfsame prized complexión.
Then please alike the pewter and the plate,
The chosen ruby and the reprobate.

In Praise of Women

O JUPITER, should I speak ill
Of womankind, first die I will;
Since that I know, 'mong all the rest
Of creatures, woman is the best.

The Delaying Bride

WHY so slowly do you move
To the centre of your love?
On your niceness though we wait,
Yet the hours say 't is late.
Coyness takes us, to a measure,
But o'eracted deads the pleasure.
Go to bed, and care not when
Cheerful day shall spring again.
One brave captain did command,
By his word, the sun to stand:
One short charm, if you but say,
Will enforce the moon to stay,
Till you warn her hence away,
T' have your blushes seen by day.

Love Discreetly

GO to your banquet then, but use delight,
So as to rise still with an appetite.
Love is a thing most nice, and must be fed
To such a height, but never surfeited.

What is beyond the mean is ever ill:
'T is best to feed love, but not over-fill.
Go then discreetly to the bed of pleasure,
And this remember, Virtue keeps the measure.

The Maypole

THE Maypole is up,
　　Now give me the cup,
I'll drink to the garlands around it;
　　But first unto those
　　Whose hands did compose
The glory of flowers that crowned it.

　　A health to my girls,
　　Whose husbands may Earls
Or Lords be (granting my wishes),
　　And when that ye wed
　　To the bridal bed,
Then multiply all like to fishes.

The Eye

A WANTON and lascivious eye
Betrays the heart's adultery.

A Song

BURN, or drown me; choose ye whether,
So I may but die together:
Thus to slay me by degrees,
Is the height of cruelties.
What needs twenty stabs when one
Strikes me dead as any stone?
O show mercy then, and be
Kind at once to murder me.

Maids' Nays Are Nothing

MAIDS' nays are nothing; they are shy
But to desire what they deny.

To Love

I'M free from thee, and thou no more shalt hear
My puling pipe to beat against thine ear:
Farewell my shackles, though of pearl they be:
Such precious thraldom ne'er shall fetter me.
He loves his bonds, who, when the first are broke,
Submits his neck unto a second yoke.

On Himself: 1

YOUNG I was, but now am old,
But I am not yet grown cold;
I can play, and I can twine
'Bout a virgin like a vine:
In her lap, too, I can lie
Melting, and in fancy die,
And return to life, if she
Claps my cheek, or kisseth me.
Thus and thus it now appears
That our love outlasts our years.

On Himself: 2

LOVESICK I am, and must endure
A desperate grief that finds no cure.
Ah me! I try and, trying, prove
No herbs have power to cure love.
Only one sovereign salve I know,
And that is death, the end of woe.

On Himself: 3

MOP-EYED I am, as some have said,
Because I've lived so long a maid:
But grant that I should wedded be,
Should I a jot the better see?
No, I should think that marriage might,
Rather than mend, put out the light.

The Suspicion Upon His Overmuch Familiarity With a Gentlewoman

AND must we part, because some say
Loud is our love, and loose our play,
And more than well becomes the day?
Alas for pity! and for us
Most innocent, and injured thus.
Had we kept close, or played within,
Suspicion now had been the sin,
And shame had followed long ere this,

T' have plagued what now unpunished is.
But we, as fearless of the sun
As faultless, will not wish undone
What now is done, since where no sin

Unbolts the door, no shame comes in.
Then, comely and most fragrant maid,
Be you more wary than afraid
Of these reports; because you see
The fairest most suspected be.
The common forms have no one eye
Or ear of burning jealousy
To follow them: but chiefly where
Love makes the cheek and chin a sphere
To dance and play in, trust me, there
Suspicion questions every hair.

Come, you are fair, and should be seen
While you are in your sprightful green.
And what though you had been embraced
By me, were you for that unchaste?
No, no, no more than is yond' moon,
Which, shining in her perfect noon,
In all that great and glorious light,
Continues cold as is the night.
Then, beauteous maid, you may retire:
And as for me, my chaste desire
Shall move t'wards you, although I see
Your face no more: so live you free
From Fame's black lips, as you from me.

The Cruel Maid

AND, cruel maid, because I see
You scornful of my love and me,
I'll trouble you no more; but go
My way, where you shall never know
What is become of me. There I
Will find me out a path to die,
Or learn some way how to forget
You and your name forever. Yet
Ere I go hence, know this from me,
What will in time your fortune be:
This to your coyness I will tell,
And, having spoke it once, farewell.
The lily will not long endure,
Nor the snow continue pure:
The rose, the violet,—one day
See! both these lady-flowers decay:
And you must fade as well as they.
And it may chance that love may turn,
And, like to mine, make your heart burn
And weep to see 't; yet this thing do,
That my last vow commends to you.
When you shall see that I am dead,
For pity let a tear be shed;
And, with your mantle o'er me cast,
Give my cold lips a kiss at last.
If twice you kiss, you need not fear
That I shall stir, or live more here.
Next, hollow out a tomb to cover
Me; me, the most despiséd lover:
And write thereon, "This, Reader, know!
Love killed this man." No more but so.

The Beggar

SHALL I a daily beggar be,
For love's sake asking alms of thee?
Still shall I crave, and never get
A hope of my desired bit?
O cruel maids! I'll go my way,
Whereas (perchance) my fortunes may
Find out a threshold or a door,
That may far sooner speed the poor:
Where thrice we knock, and none will hear,
Cold comfort still (I'm sure) lives there.

Prince of Love

LOVE like a gypsy lately came,
  And did me much importune
To see my hand, that by the same
  He might foretell my fortune.

He saw my palm; and then said he,
  I tell thee, by this score here,
That thou within few months shalt be
  The youthful Prince d'Amour here.

I smiled, and bade him once more prove,
  And by some cross-line show it,
That I could ne'er be Prince of Love,
  Though here the princely poet.

Upon Some Women

THOU who wilt not love, do this—
Learn of me what woman is:
Something made of thread and thrum,[1]
A mere botch of all and some;
Pieces, patches, ropes of hair,
Inlaid garbage ev'rywhere;
Outside silk, and outside lawn,
Scenes to cheat us neatly drawn;
False in legs, and false in thighs;
False in breast, teeth, hair, and eyes;
False in head, and false enough,
Only true in shreds and stuff.

A Song to the Maskers

COME down, and dance ye in the toil
    Of pleasures to a heat:
But if to moisture, let the oil
    Of roses be your sweat.

Not only to yourselves assume
    These sweets, but let them fly
From this to that, and so perfume
    E'en all the standers-by:

As goddess Isis, when she went,
    Or glided through the street,
Made all that touched her, with her scent,
    And whom she touched turn sweet.

[1] Thrum: waste shreds or bits of yarn.

The Wounded Heart

COME bring your sampler, and with art
  Draw in 't a wounded heart
  And dropping here and there:
Not that I think that any dart
  Can make yours bleed a tear,
  Or pierce it anywhere.
Yet do it to this end, that I,
          Maybe
            This secret see,
      Though you can make
That heart to bleed, yours ne'er will ache
        For me.

No Loathsomeness in Love

WHAT I fancy, I approve:
No dislike there is in love.
Be my mistress short or tall,
And distorted therewithal:
Be she likewise one of those,
That an acre hath of nose:
Be her forehead and her eyes
Full of incongruities:
Be her cheeks so shallow too,
As to show her tongue wag through:
Be her lips ill hung or set,
And her grinders black as jet:
Has she thin hair, hath she none,
She's to me a paragon!

His Answer to a Question

SOME would know
   Why I so
Long still do tarry,
   And ask why
   Here that I
Live, and not marry.
   Thus I those
   Do oppose:
What man would be here
   Slave to thrall,
   If at all
He could live free here?

Love Killed by Lack

LET me be warm, let me be fully fed:
Luxurious love by wealth is nourishéd.
Let me be lean, and cold, and once grown poor,
I shall dislike what once I loved before.

Love's Play at Push-Pin

LOVE and myself (believe me) on a day
At childish push-pin for our sport did play:
I put, he pushed, and heedless of my skin,
Love pricked my finger with a golden pin:
Since which, it festers so, that I can prove
'T was but a trick to poison me with love.
Little the wound was; greater was the smart;
The finger bled, but burnt was all my heart.

A Hymn to the Graces

WHEN I love, (as some have told,
Love I shall when I am old)
O ye Graces! Make me fit
For the welcoming of it.
Clean my rooms as temples be,
T' entertain that Deity.
Give me words wherewith to woo,
Suppling and successfull too:
Winning postures; and withal,
Manners each way musical;
Sweetness to allay my sour,
And unsmooth behaviour.
For I know you have the skill
Vines to prune, though not to kill,
And of any wood ye see,
You can make a Mercury.

The Bag of the Bee

ABOUT the sweet bag of a bee,
    Two Cupids fell at odds;
And whose the pretty prize should be,
    They vowed to ask the Gods.

Which, Venus hearing, thither came,
    And for their boldness stripped them;
And, taking thence from each his flame,
    With rods of myrtle whipped them.

Which done, to still their wanton cries,
    When quite grown she'd seen them,
She kissed, and wiped their dove-like eyes;
    And gave the bag between them.

The Present: or, The Bag of the Bee

FLY to my mistress, pretty pilf'ring Bee,
And say, thou bring'st this honeybag from me:
When on her lip, thou hast thy sweet dew placed,
Mark, if her tongue, but slyly, steal a taste.
If so, we live; if not, with mournful hum,
Toll forth my death; next, to my burial come.

The Frozen Heart

I FREEZE, I freeze, and nothing dwells
In me but snow, and icicles.
For pity's sake give your advice,
To melt this snow, and thaw this ice;
I'll drink down flames, but if so be
Nothing but love can supple me;
I'll rather keep this frost, and snow,
Then to be thawed or heated so.

The Hourglass

THAT hourglass, which there ye see
With water filled, (Sirs, credit me)
The humor was, as I have read,
But lovers' tears encrystalléd,
Which, as they drop by drop do pass
From the upper to the under glass,
Do in a trickling manner tell,
(By many a watery syllable),
That lovers' tears in lifetime shed,
Do restless run when they are dead.

The Good-Night, or Blessing

BLESSINGS, in abundance come,
To the bride, and to her groom;
May the bed, and this short night,
Know the fullness of delight!
Pleasures, many here attend ye,
And ere long, a boy love send ye
Curled and comely, and so trim,
Maids in time may ravish him.
Thus a dew of graces fall
On ye both. Good-night to all.

To All Young Men That Love

I COULD wish you all, who love,
That ye could your thoughts remove
From your mistresses, and be,
Wisely wanton like to me.
I could wish you dispossessed
Of that fiend that mars your rest;
And with tapers comes to fright
Your weak senses in the night.

I could wish, ye all, who fry
Cold as ice, or cool as I.
But if flames best like ye, then
Much good do 't ye Gentlemen.
I a merry heart will keep,
While you wring your hands and weep.

Love Dislikes Nothing

WHATSOEVER thing I see,
Rich or poor although it be;
'T is a mistress unto me.

Be my girl, or fair or brown,
Does she smile, or does she frown:
Still I write a sweetheart down.

Be she rough, or smooth of skin;
When I touch, I then begin
For to let affection in.

Be she bald, or does she wear
Locks incurled of other hair;
I shall find enchantment there.

Be she whole, or be she rent,
So my fancy be content,
She's to me most excellent.

Be she fat, or be she lean,
Be she sluttish, be she clean,
I'm a man for every scene.

The Definition of Beauty

BEAUTY no other thing is than a beam
Flashed out between the middle and extreme.

His Recantation

LOVE, I recant,
And pardon crave
That lately I offended,
But 'twas,
Alas!
To make a brave,
But no disdain intended.

No more I'll vaunt,
For now I see,
Thou only hast the power
To find
And bind
A heart that's free,
And slave it in an hour.

Leander's Obsequies

WHEN as Leander young was drowned,
No heart by love received a wound;
But on a rock himself sat by,
There weeping sup'rabundantly.
Sighs numberless he cast about,
And all his tapers thus put out:
His head upon his hand he laid;
And sobbing deeply, thus he said,
Ah, cruel sea! and looking on 't,
Wept as he'd drown the Hellespont.
And sure his tongue had more expressed,
But that his tears forbade the rest.

The Bondman

BIND me but to thee with thine hair,
    And quickly I shall be
Made by that fetter or that snare
    A bondman unto thee.

Or if thou tak'st that bond away,
    Then bore me through the ear;
And by the law I ought to stay
    Forever with thee here.

The Kiss: A Dialogue

1. AMONG thy fancies, tell me this:
   What is the thing we call a kiss?
2. I shall resolve thee what it is.
   It is a creature born and bred

   Between the lips, all cherry-red,
   By love and warm desires fed:
Chor. And makes more soft the bridal bed.

2. It is an active flame that flies
   First to the babies of the eyes,
   And charms them there with lullabies:
Chor. And stills the bride too when she cries.

2. Then to the chin, the cheek, the ear,
   It frisks, and flies, now here, now there,
   'T is now far off, and then 't is near:
Chor. And here, and there, and everywhere.

1. Has it a speaking virtue? 2. Yes.
1. How speaks it, say? 2. Do you but this:
   Part your joined lips, then speaks your kiss.
Chor. And this love's sweetest language is.

1. Has it a body? 2. Aye, and wings,
   With thousand rare encolorings;
   And as it flies, it gently sings,
Chor. Love honey yields, but never stings.

Long and Lazy

THAT was the proverb. Let my mistress be
Lazy to others, but be long to me.[1]

No Fault in Women

NO fault in women to refuse
The offer which they most would choose:
No fault in women to confess
How tedious they are in their dress:
No fault in women to lay on
The tincture of vermillion,
And there to give their cheek a dye
Of white, where nature doth deny:
No fault in women to make show
Of largeness, when th' are nothing so;
When true it is the outside swells
With inward buckram, little else:
No fault in women, though they be
But seldom from suspicion free:
No fault in womankind at all.
If they but slip, and never fall.

[1] The proverb is obscure, but the pun is obvious.

To Virgins

HEAR, ye virgins, and I'll teach
What the times of old did preach.
Rosamond was in a bower
Kept, as Danae in a tower:
But yet love, who subtle is,
Crept to that, and came to this.
Be ye locked up like to these,
Or the rich Hesperides;
Or those babies in your eyes,
In their crystal nunneries:
Notwithstanding love will win,
Or else force, a passage in;
And as coy be, as you can,
Gifts will get ye, or the man.

Dissuasions From Idleness

CYNTHIUS pluck ye by the ear,
That ye may good doctrine hear.
Play not with the maiden-hair;
For each ringlet there's a snare.
Cheek, and eye, and lip, and chin;
These are traps to take fools in.
Arms, and hands, and all parts else,
Are but toils, or manacles
Set on purpose to enthrall
Men, but slothfulls most of all.
Live employed, and so live free
From these fetters; like to me
Who have found, and still can prove,
The lazy man the most doth love.

Not to Love

HE that will not love, must be
My scholar, and learn this of me:
There be in love as many fears
As the summer's corn has ears;
Sighs, and sobs, and sorrows more
Than the sand that makes the shore;
Freezing cold, and fiery heats,
Fainting swoons, and deadly sweats;
Now an ague, then a fever,
Both tormenting lovers ever.
Would'st thou know, besides all these,
How hard a woman 't is to please?
How cross, how sullen, and how soon
She shifts and changes like the moon;
How false, how hollow she's in heart;
And how she is her own least part:
How high she's prized, and worth but small? —
Little thou 'llt love, or not at all.

I Call and I Call

I CALL, I call. Who do ye call?
The maids to catch this cowslip-ball.
But since these cowslips fading be,
Troth, leave the flowers, and maids, take me.
Yet if that neither you will do,
Speak but the word, and I'll take you.

Love Lightly Pleased

LET fair or foul my mistress be,
Or low, or tall, she pleaseth me.
Or let her walk, or stand or sit, —
The posture hers, I'm pleased with it.
Or let her tongue be still, or stir,
Graceful is everything from her.
Or let her grant, or else deny,
My love will fit each history.

To the Most Fair and Lovely Mistress, Anne Soame

SO smell those odors that do rise
From out the wealthy spiceries;
So smells the flower of blooming clove,
Or roses smother'd in the stove;
So smells the air of spicéd wine,
Or essences of jessamine;
So smells the breath about the hives,
When well the work of honey thrives,
And all the busy factors come
Laden with wax and honey home;
So smell those neat and woven bowers,
All over-arched with orange flowers
And almond blossoms, that do mix
To make rich these aromatics:
So smell those bracelets, and those bands
Of amber chafed between the hands,
When thus enkindled they transpire
A noble perfume from the fire.
The smell of morning milk and cream,
Butter of cowslips mixed with them,
Of roasted warden, or baked pear,
These are not be reckoned here,
When as the meanest part of her
Smells like the maiden-pomander. —
Thus sweet she smells, or what can be
More liked by her, or loved by me.

An Epitaph Upon a Virgin

HERE a solemn fast we keep,
While all beauty lies asleep:
Hushed be all things; no noise here,
But the toning of a tear,
Or a sigh of such as bring
Cowslips for her covering.

Impossibilities: To His Friend

MY faithful friend, if you can see
The fruit to grow up, or the tree.
If you can see the color come
Into the blushing pear or plum,
If you can see the water grow
To cakes of ice or flakes of snow,
If you can see that drop of rain
Lost in the wild sea, once again,
If you can see how dreams do creep
Into the brain by easy sleep:
Then there is hope that you may see
Her love me once who now hates me.

Lips Tongueless

FOR my part, I never care
For those lips that tongue-tied are:
Tell-tales I would have them be
Of my mistress and of me.
Let them prattle how that I
Sometimes freeze and sometimes fry;
Let them tell how she doth move
Fore or backward in her love;
Let them speak by gentle tones,
One and th' other's passións:
How we watch, and seldom sleep;
How by willows we do weep;
How by stealth we meet, and then
Kiss, and sigh, so part again: —
This the lips we will permit
For to tell, not publish it.

Upon a Delaying Lady

COME, come away,
Or let me go;
Must I here stay,
Because y' are slow,
And will continue so?
Troth, lady, no.

I scorn to be
A slave to state:
And since I'm free,
I will not wait
Henceforth at such a rate,
For needy fate.

If you desire
My spark should glow,
The peeping fire
You must blow;
Or I shall quickly grow
To frost or snow.

Clothes Do But Cheat and Cozen Us

AWAY with silks, away with lawn;
I'll have no screens or curtains drawn.
Give me my mistress, as she is,
Dressed in her naked simplicities:
For as my heart, e'en so mine eye,
Is won with flesh, not drapery.

To the Water Nymphs Drinking
at the Fountain

REACH with your whiter hands to me
　　Some crystal of the spring,
And I about the cup shall see
　　Fresh lilies flourishing.

Or else sweet nymphs, do you but this—
　　To' th' glass your lips incline;
And I shall see, by that one kiss,
　　The water turned to wine.

A Nuptial Song, or Epithalamy,
on Sir Clipseby Crew and His Lady

WHAT'S that we see from far? the spring of day
Bloomed from the east, or fair bejewelled May
　　Blown out of April; or some new
　　Star filled with glory to our view,
　　　　Reaching at heaven,
To add a noble planet to the seven?
　　Say, or do we not descry
Some goddess, in a cloud of tiffany
　　　　To move, or rather the
　　Emergent Venus from the sea?

'T is she! 't is she! or else some more divine
Enlightened substance; mark how from the shrine
　　Of holy saints she paces on,

Treading upon vermilion
         And amber; spice-
ing the chaste air with fumes of paradise.
     Then come on, come on, and yield
A favor like unto a blessèd field,
         When the bedabbled morn
     Washes the golden ears of corn.

See where she comes; and smell how all the street
Breathes vineyards and pomegranates: O how sweet!
     As a fired altar is each stone,
     Perspiring pounded cinnamon.
              The phoenix nest,
Built up of odors, burneth in her breast.
     Who therein would not consume
His soul to ash-heaps in that rich perfume?
         Bestroking fate the while
     He burns to embers on the pile.

Hymen! O Hymen! tread the sacred ground,
Show thy white feet, and head with marjoram crowned:
     Mount up thy flames, and let thy torch
     Display the bridegroom in the porch,
              In his desires
More towering, more sparkling than thy fires:
     Show her how his eyes do turn
And roll about, and in their motions burn
         Their balls to cinders: haste,
     Or else to ashes he will waste.

Glide by the banks of virgins then, and pass
The showers of roses, lucky four-leaved grass;
     The while the cloud of younglings sing,

And drown ye with a flowery spring:
       While some repeat
Your praise, and bless you, sprinkling you with wheat;
       While that others do divine
Blest is the bride on whom the sun doth shine;
       And thousands gladly wish
       You multiply as doth a fish.

And beauteous bride, we do confess y' are wise
In dealing forth these bashful jealousies:
       In love's name do so, and a price
       Set on your self, by being nice.
              But yet take heed;
What now you seem, be not the same indeed,
       And turn apostate: love will
Part of the way be met, or sit stonestill.
              On then, and though
       You slowly go, yet, howsoever, go.

And now y' are enter'd. See the coddled cook
Runs from his torrid zone to pry and look,
       And bless his dainty mistress: see
       The aged point out, this is she,
              Who now must sway
The house, love shield her! with her yea and nay:
       And the smirk butler thinks it
Sin, in 's napery not to express his wit;
       Each striving to devise
       Some gin wherewith to catch your eyes.

To bed, to bed, kind turtles, now, and write
This the short'st day and this the longest night;
       But yet too short for you: 't is we,

Who count this night as long as three,
    Lying alone,
Telling the clock strike ten, eleven, twelve, one,
    Quickly, quickly then prepare;
And let the young men and the bridemaids share
    Your garters, and their joints
    Encircle with the bridegroom's points.

By the bride's eyes, and by the teeming life
Of her green hopes, we charge ye that no strife,
    Farther than gentleness tends, gets place
    Among ye, striving for her lace:
        O do not fall
Foul in these noble pastimes, lest ye call
    Discord in, and so divide
The youthful bridegroom and the fragrant bride:
    (Which love forefend!) but spoken
    Be 't to your praise, no peace was broken.

Strip her of springtime, tender whimpering maids,
Now autumn's come, when all those flowery aids
    Of her delays must end. Dispose
    That lady-smock, that pansy, and that rose
        Neatly apart;
But for prick-madam, and for gentleheart,
    And soft maiden's-blush, the bride
Makes holy these, all others lay aside:
        Then strip her, or unto her
    Let him come who dares undo her.

And to enchant ye more, see everywhere
About the roof a siren in a sphere,
    As we think, singing to the din

Of many a warbling cherubim.
　　O mark ye how
The soul of nature melts in numbers: now
　　See, a thousand cupids fly,
To light their tapers at the bride's bright eye.
　　To bed, or her they'll tire.
Were she an element of fire.

And to your more bewitching, see the proud
Plump bed bear up and swelling like a cloud,
　　Tempting the two too modest. Can
　　Ye see it brustle like a swan,
　　　　And you be cold
To meet it, when it woos and seems to fold
　　The arms to hug it? Throw, throw
Yourselves into the mighty overflow
　　　　Of that white pride, and drown
　　The night with you in floods of down.

The bed is ready, and the maze of love
Looks for the treaders. Everywhere is wove
　　Wit and new mystery; read, and
　　Put in practice, to understand
　　　　And know each wile,
Each hieroglyphic of a kiss or smile,
　　And do it to the full; reach
High in your own conceit, and some way teach
　　Nature and art one more
　　Play than they ever knew before.

If needs we must for ceremony's sake,
Bless a sack-posset, luck go with it: take
　　The night-charm quickly; you have spells

And magics for to end, and hells
    To pass; but such,
And of such torture, as no one would grudge
    To live therein forever, fry
And consume, and grow again to die,
        And live, and in that case,
    Love the confusion of the place.

But since it must be done, dispatch, and sow
Up in a sheet your bride: and what if so
    It be with rock, or walls of brass,
    Ye tower her up, as Danae was?
        Think you that this,
Or hell itself a powerful bulwark is?
    I tell ye no; but like a
Bold bolt of thunder he will make his way,
        And rend the cloud, and throw
    The sheet about like flakes of snow.

All now is hushed in silence. Midwife-moon,
With all her owl-eyed issue, begs a boon
    Which you must grant,—that's entrance; with
    Which extract, all we can call pith
        And quintessence
Of planetary bodies: so commence
    All fair constellations,
Looking upon ye, that, that nations,
      Springing from two such fires,
    May blaze the virtue of their sires.

Upon His Kinswoman
Mistress Bridget Herrick

SWEET Bridget blushed, and therewithal,
Fresh blossoms from her cheeks did fall.
I thought at first 't was but a dream,
Till after I had handled them,
And smelt them, then they smelt to me,
As blossoms of the almond tree.

His Parting From Mrs. Dorothy Keneday

WHEN I did go from thee, I felt that smart,
Which bodies do, when souls from them depart.

Thou did'st not mind it; though thou then might'st see
Me turned to tears; yet did'st not weep for me.

'T is true, I kissed thee; but I could not hear
Thee spend a sigh, t' accompany my tear.

Methought 't was strange, that thou so hard should'st prove
Whose heart, whose hand, whose every part spake love.

Prithee, lest maids should censure thee, but say
Thou shedd'st one tear, when as I went away;

And that will please me somewhat: though I know,
And Love will swear't, my Dearest did not so.

Mrs. Eliz. Wheeler, Under the Name of The Lost Shepherdess

AMONG the myrtles, as I walked,
Love and my sighs thus intertalked,
Tell me, said I, in deep distress,
Where I may find my shepherdess.
Thou fool, said Love, know'st thou not this?
In every thing that's sweet, she is.
In yond' carnation go and seek,
There thou shalt find her lip and cheek:
In that enamelled pansy by,
There thou shalt have her curious eye:
In bloom of peach, and roses' bud,
There waves the streamer of her blood.
'T is true, said I, and thereupon
I went to pluck them one by one,
To make of parts an union;
But on a sudden all were gone.
At which I stopped. Said Love: These be
The true resemblances of thee;
For as these flowers, thy joys must die,
And in the turning of an eye;
And all thy hopes of her must wither,
Like those short sweets ere knit together.

A Hymn to Venus and Cupid

SEA-BORN Goddess, let me be,
By thy son thus graced, and thee;
That whene'er I woo, I find
Virgins coy, but not unkind.
Let me when I kiss a maid,
Taste her lips, so overlaid
With Love's syrup, that I may,
In your temple, when I pray,
Kiss the altar, and confess
There's in love no bitterness.

A Short Hymn to Venus

GODDESS, I do love a girl
Ruby-lipped and toothed with pearl:
If so be, I may but prove
Lucky in this maid I love,
I will promise there shall be
Myrtles offered up to thee.

A Vow to Venus

HAPPILY I had a sight
Of my dearest dear last night;
Make her this day smile on me,
And I'll roses give to thee.

Upon Cupid: 1

OLD wives have often told how they
Saw Cupid bitten by a flea;
And thereupon, in tears half drowned,
He cried aloud, "Help, help the wound."
He wept, he sobbed, he called to some
To bring him lint and balsamum,
To make a tent, and put it in
Where the stiletto pierced the skin:
Which being done, the fretful pain
Assuaged, and he was well again.

Upon Cupid: 2

AS lately I a garland bound,
'Mongst roses, I there Cupid found:
I took him, put him in my cup,
And, drunk with wine, I drank him up.
Hence then it is, that my poor breast
Could never since find any rest.

Upon Cupid: 3

LOVE like a beggar came to me
    With hose and doublet torn;
His shirt bedangling from his knee,
    With hat and shoes outworn.

He asked an alms; I gave him bread,
    And meat too for his need;
Of which when he had fully fed,
    He wished me all good speed.

Away he went; but as he turned,
    In faith I know not how,
He touched me so, as that I burn
    And am tormented now.

Love's silent flames and fires obscure
    Then crept into my heart;
And though I saw no bow, I'm sure
    His finger was the dart.

The Cheat of Cupid:
or, The Ungentle Guest

ONE silent night of late,
    When every creature rested,
Came one unto my gate,
    And knocking, me molested.

Who's that, said I, beats there,
    And troubles thus the sleepy?
Cast off, said he, all fear,
    And let not locks thus keep ye.

For I a boy am, who
    By moonless nights have swerved;
And all with showers wet through,
    And e'en with cold half starved.

I pitiful arose,
    And soon a taper lighted;
And did myself disclose
    Unto the lad benighted.

I saw he had a bow,
    And wings too, which did shiver;
And looking down below,
    I spied he had a quiver.

I to my chimney's shine
    Brought him, as love professes,
And chafed his hands with mine,
    And dried his dropping tresses.

But when he felt him warmed,
   Let's try this bow of ours
And string, if they be harmed,
   Said he, with these late showers.

Forthwith his bow he bent,
   And wedded string and arrow,
And struck me that it went
   Quite through my heart and marrow.

Then laughing loud, he flew
   Away, and thus said flying;
Adieu, mine host, adieu,
   I'll leave thy heart a dying.

A Hymn to Cupid

THOU, thou that bear'st the sway,
With whom the sea-nymphs play,
And Venus, every way;

When I embraced thy knee,
And make short prayers to thee,
In love then prosper me.

This day I go to woo;
Instruct me how to do
This work thou putt'st me to.

From shame my face keep free,
From scorn I beg of thee,
Love, to deliver me:

So shall I sing thy praise,
And to thee altars raise
Unto the end of days.

The Wounded Cupid

CUPID, as he lay among
Roses, by a bee was stung.
Whereupon, in anger flying
To his mother, said thus crying:
Help! O help! your boy's a dying.
And why, my pretty lad, said she?
Then blubbering, repliéd he,
A wingéd snake has bitten me,
Which country people call a bee.
At which she smiled; then with her hairs
And kisses drying up his tears,
Alas! said she, my wag, if this
Such a pernicious torment is,
Come tell me then, how great's the smart
Of those thou woundest with thy dart!

To Dews

I BURN, I burn, and beg of you
To quench, or cool me with your dew:
I fry in fire, and so consume,
Although the pile be all perfume.
Alas! the heat and death's the same,
Whether by choice or common flame:
To be in oil of roses drowned,
Or water, where's the comfort found?
Both bring one death, and I die here,
Unless you cool me with a tear.
Alas! I call; but ah! I see
Ye cool, and comfort all but me.

Love Me Little, Love Me Long

YOU say to me-wards your affection's strong;
Pray love me little, so you love me long.
Slowly goes far; the mean is best; desire
Grown violent, does either die, or tire.

Upon a Wife That Died
Mad with Jealousy

IN this little vault she lies,
Here, with all her jealousies:
Quiet yet; but if ye make
Any noise, they both will wake,
And such spirits raise, 'twill then
Trouble Death to lay again.

A Hymn to Love

I WILL confess
With cheerfulness,
Love is a thing so likes me,
    That let her lay
    On me all day
I'll kiss the hand that strikes me.

I will not, I,
Now blubb'ring cry
It ah! too late repents me,
    That I did fall
    To love at all,
Since love so much contents me.

No, no, I'll be
In fetters free;
While others they sit wringing
    Their hands for pain,
    I'll entertain
The wounds of love with singing.

With flowers and wine,
And cakes divine,
To strike me I will tempt thee:
    Which done, no more
    I'll come before
Thee and thine altars empty.

Comfort to a Youth That Had Lost His Love

WHAT needs complaints,
When she a place
Has with the race
    Of saints?

In endless mirth,
She thinks not on
What's said or done
    In earth.

She sees no tears,
Or any tone
Of thy deep groan
    She hears:

Nor does she mind,
Or think on 't now,
That ever thou
    Wast kind.

But changed above,
She likes not there,
As she did here,
    Thy love.

Forbear therefore,
And lull asleep
Thy woes, and weep
    No more.

The Scar-Fire

WATER, water I desire;
Here's a house of flesh on fire.
Ope the fountains and the springs,
And come all to bucketings.
What ye cannot quench, pull down.
Spoil a house to save a town;
Better 't is that one should fall,
Than by one to hazard all.

Upon Love: 1

HOW Love came in, I do not know,
Whether by th' eye, or ear, or no;
Or whether with the soul it came
At first, infuséd with the same;
Whether in part 'tis here or there,
Or, like the soul, whole everywhere.
This troubles me; but I as well
As any other, this can tell;
That when from hence she does depart,
The outlet then is from the heart.

Upon Love: 2

LOVE scorched my finger, but did spare
  The burning of my heart;
To signify, in love my share
  Should be a little part.

Little I love; but if that he
  Would but that heat recall,
That joined to ashes should be burnt,
  Ere I would love at all.

Upon Love: 3

LOVE, I have broke
  Thy yoke;
The neck is free:
But when I'm next
  Love-vexed,
Then shackle me.

'T is better yet
  To fret
The feet or hands,
Than to enthrall
  Or gall
The neck with bands.

Upon Love: 4

LOVE bade me ask a gift,
   And I no more did move,
But this, that I might shift
   Still with my clothes, my love.
That favor granted was;
   Since which, though I love many,
Yet so it comes to pass,
   That long I love not any.

Upon Love: 5

LOVE'S a thing, as I do hear,
Ever full of pensive fear:
Rather than to which I'll fall,
Trust me, I'll not like at all.
If to love I should intend,
Let my hair then stand on end,
And that terror likewise prove,
Fatal to me in my love.
But if horror cannot slake
Flames which would an entrance make,
Then the next thing I desire,
Is to love, and live in fire.

Upon Love: 6

I DO not love, nor can it be
Love will in vain spend shafts on me.
I did this god-head once defy;
Since which I freeze, but cannot fry:
Yet out, alas! the death's the same,
Killed by a frost or by a flame.

Upon Love: 7

I PLAYED with Love, as with the fire
    The wanton Satyr did;
Nor did I know or could descry
    What under there was hid.

That Satyr he but burned his lips,
    But mine's the greater smart;
For kissing Love's dissembling chips,
    The fire scorched my heart.

Upon Love: 8

    I'LL get me hence,
    Because no fence
Or fort that I can make here,
    But love by charms,
    Or else by arms,
Will storm, or, starving, take here.

Upon Love: 9

SOME salve to every sore we may apply,
Only for my wound there's no remedy:
Yet if my Julia kiss me, there will be
A sovereign balm found out to rescue me.

Upon Love: 10

LOVE brought me to a silent grove,
    And showed me there a tree
Where some had hanged themselves for love
    And gave a twist to me.

The halter was of silk and gold
    That he reached forth unto me,
No otherwise than if he would
    By dainty things undo me.

He bade me then that necklace use,
    And told me, too, he maketh
A glorious end by such a noose,
    His death for love that taketh.

'T was but a dream; but had I been
    There really alone,
My desperate fears in love had seen
    Mine executión.

Upon Love: 11

I HELD Love's head while it did ache;
    But so it chanced to be;
The cruel pain did his forsake,
    And forthwith came to me.

Ah me! How shall my grief be stilled?
    Or where else shall we find
One like to me, who must be killed
    For being too-too-kind?

To His Girls, Who Would Have Him Sportful

ALAS! I can't, for tell me how
Can I be gamesome, agéd now.
Besides, ye see me daily grow
Here, winter-like, to frost and snow;
And I ere long, my girls, shall see
Ye quake for cold to look on me.

On Fortune

THIS is my comfort, when she's most unkind;
She can but spoil me of my means, not mind.

Last Words

TO his book's end this last line he'd have placed;
Jocund his Muse was, but his life was chaste.

THE LOVE POEMS

of

JOHN DONNE

Introduction

THE LIFE of John Donne was one long struggle between spirit and flesh, between the inexplicable mystery of the soul and the revelation of the body which "is his book." The conflict was in him from the beginning. Donne could do nothing without intensity. Yet his was never a single-minded passion. He was both sensual and cynical; a prey to emotion, he was also emotion's analyst. A gallant, a soldier, man-about-town in his youth, he turned in maturity from physical delight to spiritual flagellation. In *John Donne: A Study in Discord*, Hugh I'Anson Fausset divides Donne's life neatly — perhaps a little too neatly — into four alliterative periods: The Pagan, The Penitent, The Pensioner, and The Preacher. Fausset maintains that Donne was on fire all his days, that the flame of life within him never failed, "rather it burned brighter and more lurid as emaciation heralded dissolution." Izaak Walton had already indicated Donne's progress from sense to spirit, from pagan licentiousness to asceticism and agonized purity, from a lust for life to a preoccupation with death. Walton praised this as a puritan's progress; his laudatory lines appear beneath Donne's youthful picture on the title page of an early edition of the poems:

This was for youth, strength, mirth, and wit, that time
Most count their golden age; but 'twas not thine.
Thine was thy later years, so much refined
From youth's dross, mirth, and wit; as thy pure mind
Thought (like the angels) nothing but the praise
Of thy Creator in those last, best days.
  Witness this book, thy emblem, which begins
  With Love, but ends with sighs and tears for sins.

Son of a London merchant (tradition has it that his father was an ironmonger) and a patrician who was the daughter of the poet John Heywood, "of the house of Sir Thomas More," John Donne was born in London some time in 1573. Brought up in a deeply religious home, immersed in Catholicism from boyhood, an alien Roman in a land of Reform, he felt he had the blood of martyrs in his veins. At thirty-seven he wrote about his mother's people: "No family . . . hath endured and suffered more in their persons and fortunes for obeying the teachers of Roman doctrine." As a child, he was tutored privately, well grounded in French and Latin. At eleven, he entered Hart Hall at Oxford, where he remained for two years. At fourteen, he became a student at Trinity College, Cambridge, where he devoted himself to logic, Euclid, and the Spanish mystics. From sixteen to nineteen, he studied privately, and in 1592 was admitted to Lincoln's Inn, where he pursued the study of law.

At about twenty, Donne abandoned orthodoxy. He became the traveler, pagan, cosmopolitan, and, by logic and experience, argued himself out of Catholicism. He began to write satires, enlisted for foreign service, went with Essex to Cadiz in 1596, visited the Azores, Italy, and Spain. Returning to England in his mid-twenties, Donne became secretary to Chancellor Sir Thomas Egerton, Lord Keeper of the Great Seal. It was in the Egerton household that he met Lady Egerton's niece, Anne More, daughter of Sir George More, Lieutenant of the Tower. There was a brief and passionate love affair and, when Donne was twenty-eight, a sudden and secret marriage.

Egerton was furious and dismissed Donne from his service. Donne was desperate but he did not lose his head. In a letter to his mother he summed up the situation with a combination of grimness and wit: "John Donne—Anne Donne—Undone." Harassed by debt and hounded by the fear of poverty, Donne turned to various expedients. He wrote spasmodically, composed pious epistles, as well as pamphlets against the Papists. Finally his father-in-law forgave him and set aside an allowance for the support of his family.

But the help was meager, and Donne's fortunes were at a low ebb. In his *Biathanatos* he soliloquized about suicide, the "scandalous disease of headlong dying" for which he confessed he often had "a sickly inclination." His meditations went further: "Whether it be" (he wrote in *Biathanatos*) "because I had my first breeding and conversation with men of suppressed and afflicted religion, accustomed to the despite of death, and hungry of an imagined martyrdom . . . or because my conscience ever assures me that no rebellious grudging at God's gifts nor other sinful concurrence accompanies these thoughts in me . . . methinks I have the keys of my prison in mine own hand, and no remedy presents itself so soon to my heart as mine own sword."

Donne struggled along, brooding and inactive, for thirteen years. In 1608 he tried to obtain a secretaryship in Ireland, but nothing came of it. He commended himself to various high personages for favors without success. Suddenly, when Donne was forty-one, James I induced him to take orders. The poet had put much of his energy into tracts and treatises attempting to convert Roman Catholics to the Church of England, and James made Donne his chaplain. He was ordained deacon and priest. Lincoln's Inn made him its preacher and, at forty-eight, he became Dean of St. Paul's.

Donne was now a fairly wealthy man. But he was far from a happy one. His wife, to whom, in spite of infidelities, he was passionately devoted, had died, worn out by child-bearing, after giving birth to a stillborn infant, in 1617. He withdrew from the world and gave himself frantically to preaching. Filled with remorse, Donne brooded over man's callousness and his own recklessness. He had, wrote Fausset, "dragged his wife away from ease to plunge her into poverty, and from life he had hurried her unsparingly to death." He threw himself into his sermons and tried to liberate his suffering in two series of religious sonnets, sublimations of sacred and profane love. Walton summed up this period of Donne's life eloquently: "He became crucified to the world and all those varieties, those imaginary pleas-ures, that are daily acted on that restless stage; and they were perfectly crucified to him. . . . Now grief took so full possession of his heart as to leave no place for joy. If it did it was a joy to be alone, where, like a pelican in the wilderness, he might bemoan himself without witness or restraint, and pour forth his passions like Job in the days of his affliction: 'O that I might have the desire of my heart! O that God would grant the thing I long for! For then, as the grave is become her house, so would I hasten to make it mine also, that we two might there make our beds together in the dark.' "

His health failed. A trip abroad gave him a short respite, but Donne knew he was doomed. "I fear not the hastening of my death, and yet I do fear the increase of the disease." In his early fifties he meditated much on man's precarious mortality. The meditations grew into a series of "Devo-tions" which were a cross between sermons and essays. They were presumably written to help the afflicted, yet they were not only intended for the caution and comfort of

Donne's listeners but for his own consolation. Read as a whole, the pages form a record of Donne's own illness. Each "Devotion" is preceded by a "motto" which gives it the character of a diary: "The Patient takes his bed"; "The Physician is sent for"; "I sleep not day nor night"; "From the Bells of the Church adjoining I am daily remembered of my burial in the funerals of others"; "Now this Bell tolling softly for another, says to me, Thou must die."

Although Donne buried himself in the "Devotions," he survived them by some eight years. But his vitality was ebbing—he said he had "to pay a fever every half-year as a rent for my life"—and he collapsed in his fifty-seventh year, the very year in which he was to have been made a bishop. He knew he would be a long time dying, but he prepared himself for dissolution. He had macabre fancies which grew increasingly morbid. He posed for a funereal statue which was set up in St. Paul's. He had himself painted in his shroud, his eyes shut, his lips closed, as though he were already in rigor mortis, and, when the picture was finished, he kept it at his bedside "his hourly object until his death." He died on March 31, 1631, and was survived by six of his twelve children.

III

As a poet, Donne has suffered from the extremes of praise and prejudice. Idolized in his own day, scornfully belittled in the eighteenth century, Donne has been enthusiastically rediscovered in our own time. His continual conflict between anxious hope and worldly disillusionment is as characteristic of our age as of his. It is highly significant that, more than three hundred years after his death, one of the most impassioned contemporary novels, Ernest Hemingway's *For Whom The Bell Tolls*, owes its title as well as its central faith to one of Donne's almost unnoticed "Devotions." The forgotten words of Donne's seventeenth-century sermon were charged with new meaning:

No man is an Iland, intire of itself; every man is a peece of the Continent, a part of the maine; if a Clod be washed away by the Sea, Europe is the lesse, as well as if a Promontorie were, as well as if a Manor of thy friends or of thine own were. Any man's death diminishes me, because I am involved in Mankinde. And therefore never send to know for whom the bell tolls. It tolls for thee.

In 1931, the tercentenary of the year of Donne's death, the influence of the poet was emphasized by *A Garland for John Donne* (Harvard University Press). In a prefatory note, the editor, Theodore Spencer, declared that "Donne has affected our time in more ways than one, and we owe him the debt of gratitude which any generation owes to those who have helped it to become articulate." In this commemorative symposium Mario Praz placed Donne against the background of the poetry of his time; John Hayward considered the poet as preacher; Mary Paton Ramsay examined his philosophy; Evelyn Simpson analyzed his earliest prose works, *Paradoxes and Problems,* chiefly written in Donne's twenties; George Williamson dealt with the poetry of our day in relation to Donne's metaphysics; Theodore Spencer compared Donne's straightforward style and probing spirit to the artificial conventions of his immediate predecessors; T. S. Eliot pointed out the changes in the progress of Donne's reputation, showed how Donne had enlarged the possibilities of lyric verse as no other English poet has done, and recognized him as "one of the few great reformers and preservers of the English tongue."

IV

The mutations of taste have dealt more drastically with Donne than with any other poet, with the possible exception of Pope. Dryden mixed praise and patronization when he wrote that Donne affected the "metaphysical," that, even in Donne's amorous verses, the poet "perplexed the minds of the fair sex with nice speculations of philosophy when he should engage their hearts and entertain them with the softnesses of love." The term "metaphysical" clung to Donne and was responsible for much misapprehension. When Dr. Samuel Johnson made up a category and called it the "Metaphysical School," many a reader was deterred by the thought of intellectual barriers, by a confusing fear of difficult wit and devious subtleties. For more than two centuries the enjoyment of Donne was marred by references to his "misspent learning and excessive ingenuity," his "far-fetched allusiveness," and a brilliance "which elicits amazement rather than pleasure." In *The English Poets*, a famous nineteenth-century compilation, Thomas Humphrey Ward spoke of Donne's "pyrotechnic display" and complained that "we weary of such unmitigated cleverness, such ceaseless straining after novelty and surprise." Even Edmund Gosse tempered his enthusiasm in an estimate printed as late as 1940 in the *Encyclopaedia Britannica:* "The influence of Donne upon the literature of England was singularly wide and deep, although almost wholly malign."

Yet Donne, hailed as a distinguished "ancestor" by the present generation, was immensely popular in his own day. His contemporaries admired him; the albums and commonplace books of the period are studded with his verses. Ben Jonson, who esteemed him "the first poet in the world in some things," wrote a dedicatory poem (printed in the edition of 1650) beginning: "Donne, the delight of Phoebus

and each Muse." An earlier edition (1633) contained a poem
by Joseph Marriot which Donne would have relished not
only for the pun:

> I see in his last preach'd and printed book,
> His picture in a sheet; in Paul's I look,
> And see his statue in a sheet of stone,
> And sure his body in the grave hath one.
> Those sheets present him dead; *these* if you buy,
> You have him living to eternity.

Two centuries of neglect and niggling criticism dimmed
the luster of Donne's name. Suddenly the tarnished reputa-
tion shone with a greater glow than ever. Anticipating the
rediscoverers (and, incidentally, warning against the false
enthusiasm of coterie worshippers) George Saintsbury wrote
at the beginning of the twentieth century: "Those who do
like him should either like him so much as to speak unad-
visedly with their lips, or else curb and restrain the expres-
sion of their love for fear that it should seem on that side
idolatry." Thirty years after Saintsbury heralded the re-
vival of Donne, his influence was acknowledged by modern
scholars and poets. A new generation of poets and critics
unequivocally responded to Donne's severe control and a
carelessness that was almost magnificent in its air of rich
excess, an ardor that leaped ahead of the breathlessly fol-
lowing reader. "It may be said with truth," wrote Humbert
Wolfe, "that nowhere else in the whole range of English
verse is there to be found in such abundance the raw and
glittering material of poetry." Donne's emotional tensions,
his paradoxes of skepticism and sex, his abstractions
heightened and clarified in vivid images, were reflected in
the works of such representative poets as T. S. Eliot, John
Crowe Ransom, Elinor Wylie, who borrowed a line from

Donne for the title of her last book: *Angels and Earthly Creatures*, and Edna St. Vincent Millay, whose sonnet sequence, *Fatal Interview*, owes more than its title to one of Donne's elegies.

Above all, Donne showed his followers an extraordinary fusion of sense and sensibility. He gave wit a double meaning; to a lively fancy he added a probing intelligence. His acceptance of human love and religious rapture was no less exalted for being scrupulously anatomized. He wrote aptly:

> Well died the world, that we might live to see
> This world of wit in his anatomy.

Donne broke through the conventions and perfected an idiom strikingly his own. He brought together disorganized pieces of a disordered world and arranged them in a world of clear vision; he united complexity of thought and simplicity of language. He abandoned the Elizabethan stereotypes of his day and wrote in a speech as straightforward as conversation. "The Canonization" begins with a harsh colloquialism: "For God's sake hold your tongue and let me love." Another poem, "The Sun Rising," opens with brusque directness: "Busy old fool, unruly Sun!" An angry elegy begins: "Nature's lay idiot, I taught thee to love." Tired of subterfuge and elaborate prettiness, the poet addresses an impatient poem to his mistress: "Come, madam, come, all rest my powers defy." Casually but dramatically Donne heightened the pitch of poetry with the power of common speech.

V

Donne was pre-eminently an innovator. He was a frank experimenter in form and a pioneer in a style which combined ingenuousness and ingenuity. T. S. Eliot emphasized the point. "The minor Elizabethan dramatists sometimes tormented the language," wrote Eliot. "Where the content is often quite simple, the expression is perverse. In the verse of Donne the thought is sometimes over-ingenious and perverse, but the language is always pure and simple." One of Donne's strangest poems is, at the same time, one of his most revealing. "The Flea" recounts a stock situation favored by the Elizabethan lyricists: the ardent lover, the coy lady, the pursuing gallant repulsed or, at least, held off by impregnable virtue. But Donne completely alters the tone. The image is grotesque; the implications become monstrous; the courtly metaphors have grown into coarse mockery. The conventional "flood of rubies" turns to actual blood; the elegant couch set in a blossomy bower is now the black body of a flea, whose "living walls of jet" serve as a marriage temple and a marriage bed. "The Ecstasy" is a poem of perfect epigrams in which the wit is lifted above the accumulating conceits. "The Good-Morrow" quaintly frames a universal thought in simple frankness.

Even Donne's "Divine Poems" are unique in their contradictions; they smolder and burn with his peculiar fire. In many of his religious verses the figures of speech are most violent, the sensation most inflamed. In an astonishing sonnet beginning "Batter my Heart" Donne confesses his need of God, but the religious ardor is expressed in a set of frankly sexual images. In a prolonged metaphor, the poet compares himself to a walled city that wants to open its gates to the besieger, and to a virgin who yearns to give herself but must be forced before she can make the complete surrender. Here, again, is the Elizabethan theme of the eager lover and the virginal beloved. But Donne characteristically intensifies and reverses the formula. The poet becomes the half-willing, half-resisting object; the town, the virgin body, the loving spirit must be taken ruthlessly. It is with a series of forceful paradoxes that Donne ends:

> Take me to you, imprison me, for I,
> Except you enthrall me never shall be free,
> Nor ever chaste, except you ravish me.

Donne's faults, his exaggerations and eccentricities, are obvious; but they are the faults of excess, never those of an impoverished imagination. In no poet has there been a more astounding union of ecstasy and austerity. No one has surpassed Donne in a fervor of passionate play and intellectual discipline.

Louis Untermeyer

I

Song: Go, and Catch a Falling Star

GO, and catch a falling star,
   Get with child a mandrake root,
Tell me, where all past years are,
   Or who cleft the devil's foot,
Teach me to hear mermaids singing,
   Or to keep off envy's stinging,
          And find
          What wind
Serves to advance an honest mind.

If thou be'st born to strange sights,
   Things invisible to see,
Ride ten thousand days and nights,
   Till age snow white hairs on thee,
Thou, when thou return'st, wilt tell me
All strange wonders that befell thee,
          And swear
          Nowhere
Lives a woman true, and fair.

If thou find'st one, let me know,
   Such a pilgrimage were sweet;
Yet do not, I would not go,
   Though at next door we might meet,
Though she were true, when you met her,

And last, till you write your letter,
       Yet she
       Will be
False, ere I come, to two, or three.

Song: Sweetest Love, I Do Not Go

SWEETEST love, I do not go,
   For weariness of thee,
Nor in hope the world can show
   A fitter love for me;
     But since that I
At the last must part, 't is best,
Thus to use myself in jest
   By feigned deaths to die.

Yesternight the sun went hence,
   And yet is here today;
He hath no desire nor sense,
   Nor half so short a way.
     Then fear not me,
But believe that I shall make
Speedier journeys, since I take
   More wings and spurs than he.

O how feeble is man's power,
   That if good fortune fall,
Cannot add another hour,
   Nor a lost hour recall;
     But come bad chance,
And we join to it our strength,

And we teach it art and length,
   Itself o'er us to advance.

When thou sigh'st, thou sigh'st not wind,
   But sigh'st my soul away;
When thou weep'st, unkindly kind,
   My life's blood doth decay.
     It cannot be
That thou lovest me as thou say'st,
If in thine my life thou waste,
   That art the best of me.

Let not thy divining heart
   Forethink me any ill;
Destiny may take thy part,
   And may thy fears fulfill.
     But think that we
Are but turned aside to sleep.
They who one another keep
   Alive, ne'er parted be.

The Sun Rising

BUSY old fool, unruly Sun,
   Why dost thou thus,
Through windows, and through curtains call on us?
Must to thy motions lovers' seasons run?
   Saucy, pedantic wretch, go chide
   Late schoolboys, and sour prentices,
Go tell Court-huntsmen, that the King will ride,
Call country ants to harvest offices;

Love, all alike, no season knows, nor clime,
Nor hours, days, months, which are the rags of time.

       Thy beams so reverend, and strong
       Why shouldst thou think?
I could eclipse and cloud them with a wink,
But that I would not lose her sight so long:
       If her eyes have not blinded thine,
       Look, and tomorrow late, tell me,
    Whether both th' Indias of spice and mine
Be where thou left'st them, or lie here with me.
Ask for those Kings whom thou saw'st yesterday,
And thou shalt hear, All here in one bed lay.

       She's all States, and all Princes, I,
       Nothing else is.
Princes do but play us; compared to this,
All honor's mimic; all wealth alchemy.
       Thou, Sun, art half as happy as we,
       In that the world's contracted thus;
    Thine age asks ease, and since thy duties be
    To warm the world, that's done in warming us.
Shine here to us, and thou art everywhere;
This bed thy center is, these walls, thy sphere.

The Good-Morrow

I WONDER, by my troth, what thou and I
Did, till we loved? Were we not weaned till then?
But sucked on country pleasures, childishly?
Or snorted we in the Seven Sleepers' den?
'T was so; but this, all pleasures fancies be;
If ever any beauty I did see,
Which I desired, and got, 't was but a dream of thee.

And now good-morrow to our waking souls,
Which watch not one another out of fear;
For love all love of other sights controls,
And makes one little room an everywhere.
Let sea-discoverers to new worlds have shown;
Let us possess one world; each hath one, and is one.

My face in thine eye, thine in mine appears,
And true plain hearts do in the faces rest;
Where can we find two better hemispheres
Without sharp north, without declining west?
Whatever dies, was not mixed equally;
If our two loves be one, or thou and I
Love so alike that none can slacken, none can die.

The Anniversary

ALL Kings, and all their favorites,
    All glory of honors, beauties, wits,
The Sun itself, which makes times, as they pass,
Is elder by a year, now, than it was

When thou and I first one another saw:
All other things to their destruction draw,
   Only our love hath no decay;
This, no tomorrow hath, nor yesterday,
Running it never runs from us away,
But truly keeps his first, last, everlasting day.

   Two graves must hide thine and my corse,
   If one might, death were no divorce.
Alas, as well as other Princes, we,
(Who Prince enough in one another be,)
Must leave at last in death, these eyes, and ears,
Oft fed with true oaths, and with sweet salt tears;
   But souls where nothing dwells but love
(All other thoughts being inmates) then shall prove
This, or a love increaséd there above,
When bodies to their graves, souls from their graves
   remove.

   And then we shall be th'roughly blest,
   But we no more, than all the rest;
Here upon earth, we're Kings, and none but we
Can be such Kings, nor of such subjects be.
Who is so safe as we? where none can do
Treason to us, except one of us two.
   True and false fears let us refrain,
Let us love nobly, and live, and add again
Years and years unto years, till we attain
To write threescore: this is the second of our reign.

The Ecstasy

WHERE, like a pillow on a bed,
   A pregnant bank swelled up, to rest
The violet's reclining head,
   Sat we two, one another's best.

Our hands were firmly cementéd
   With a fast balm, which thence did spring,
Our eye-beams twisted, and did thread
   Our eyes, upon one double string;

So t' intergraft our hands, as yet
   Was all the means to make us one,
And pictures in our eyes to get
   Was all our propagatión.

As 'twixt two equal armies, Fate
   Suspends uncertain victory,
Our souls (which to advance their state,
   Were gone out), hung 'twixt her, and me.

And whilst our souls negotiate there,
   We like sepulchral statues lay;
All day, the same our postures were,
   And we said nothing, all the day.

If any, so by love refined,
   That he soul's language understood,
And by good love were grown all mind,
   Within convenient distance stood,

He (though he knew not which soul spake,
   Because both meant, both spake the same)
Might thence a new concoction take,
   And part far purer than he came.

This ecstasy doth unperplex
   (We said) and tell us what we love,
We see by this, it was not sex,
   We see, we saw not what did move:

But as all several souls contain
   Mixture of things, they know not what,
Love these mixed souls doth mix again,
   And makes both one, each this and that.

A single violet transplant,
   The strength, the color, and the size,
(All which before was poor, and scant),
   Redoubles still, and multiplies.

When love, with one another so
   Inter-inanimates two souls,
That abler soul, which thence doth flow,
   Defects of loneliness controls.

We then, who are this new soul, know,
   Of what we are composed, and made,
For, th' Atomies of which we grow,
   Are souls, whom no change can invade.

But O alas, so long, so far
   Our bodies why do we forbear?
They are ours, though they are not we. We are
   The intelligences, they the spheres.

We owe them thanks, because they thus,
  Did us, to us, at first convey,
Yielded their forces, sense, to us,
  Nor are dross to us, but allay.

On man heaven's influence works not so,
  But that it first imprints the air,
So soul into the soul may flow,
  Though it to body first repair.

As our blood labors to beget
  Spirits, as like souls as it can,
Because such fingers need to knit
  That subtle knot, which makes us man:

So must pure lovers' souls descend
  T' affections, and to faculties,
Which sense may reach and apprehend,
  Else a great Prince in prison lies.

To our bodies turn we then, that so
  Weak men on love revealed may look;
Love's mysteries in souls do grow,
  But yet the body is his book,

And if some lover, such as we,
  Have heard this dialogue of one,
Let him still mark us, he shall see
  Small change, when we're to bodies gone.

The Canonization

FOR God's sake hold your tongue, and let me love;
  Or chide my palsy, or my gout,
My five grey hairs, or ruined fortune flout;
  With wealth your state, your mind with arts improve,
    Take you a course, get you a place,
    Observe his Honor, or his Grace,
Or the King's real, or his stamped face
  Contemplate; what you will, approve,
  So you will let me love.

Alas, alas, who's injured by my love?
  What merchant's ships have my sighs drowned?
Who says my tears have overflowed his ground?
  When did my colds a forward spring remove?
    When did the heats which my veins fill
    Add one more to the plaguy bill?
Soldiers find wars, and lawyers find out still
  Litigious men, which quarrels move,
  Though she and I do love.

Call us what you will, we are made such by love;
  Call her one, me another fly,
We're tapers too, and at our own cost die,
  And we in us find the Eagle and the Dove.
    The Phœnix riddle hath more wit
    By us; we two being one, are it.
So to one neutral thing both sexes fit,
  We die and rise the same, and prove
  Mysterious by this love.

We can die by it, if not live by love,
   And if unfit for tombs and hearse
Our legend be, it will be fit for verse;
    And if no piece of Chronicle we prove,
      We'll build in sonnets pretty rooms;
      As well a well-wrought urn becomes
The greatest ashes as half-acre tombs,
   And by these hymns, all shall approve
   Us canonized for Love:

And thus invoke us: You whom reverend love
   Made one another's hermitage;
You, to whom love was peace that now is rage;
    Who did the whole world's soul contract, and drove
      Into the glasses of your eyes
      (So much made mirrors and such spies
That they did all to you epitomize),
   Countries, towns, courts—beg from above
   A pattern of your love!

Love's Deity

I LONG to talk with some old lover's ghost,
  Who died before the god of love was born.
I cannot think that he, who then loved most,
  Sunk so low as to love one which did scorn.
But since this god produced a destiny,
And that vice-nature, custom, lets it be,
  I must love her that loves not me.

Sure, they which made him god, meant not so much,
  Nor he in his young godhead practised it.
But when an even flame two hearts did touch,
  His office was indulgently to fit
Actives to passives. Correspondency
Only his subject was; it cannot be
  Love, till I love her, who loves me.

But every modern god will now extend
  His vast prerogative as far as Jove.
To rage, to lust, to write to, to commend,
  All is the purlieu of the god of love.
O! were we wakened by this tyranny
To ungod this child again, it could not be
  I should love her, who loves not me.

Rebel and atheist too, why murmur I,
  As though I felt the worst that love could do?
Love may make me leave loving, or might try
  A deeper plague, to make her love me too;
Which, since she loves before, I'm loth to see.
Falsehood is worse than hate; and that must be,
  If she whom I love, should love me.

Love's Diet

TO what a cumbersome unwieldiness
And burdenous corpulence my love had grown,
   But that I did, to make it less,
   And keep it in propórtión,
Give it a diet, made it feed upon
That which love worst endures, discretión.

Above one sigh a day I allowed him not,
Of which my fortune, and my faults had part;
   And if sometimes by stealth he got
   A she sigh from my mistress' heart,
And thought to feast on that, I let him see
'T was neither very sound, nor meant to me.

If he wrung from me a tear, I brined it so
With scorn or shame, that him it nourished not;
   If he sucked hers, I let him know
   'T was not a tear which he had got;
His drink was counterfeit, as was his meat;
For eyes, which roll towards all, weep not, but sweat.

Whatever he would dictate I writ that,
But burnt her letters when she writ to me;
   And if that favor made him fat,
   I said, "If any title be
Conveyed by this, ah! what doth it avail,
To be the fortieth name in an entail?"

Thus I reclaimed my buzzard love, to fly
At what, and when, and how, and where I choose.

Now negligent of sports I lie,
    And now, as other falconers use,
I spring a mistress, swear, write, sigh, and weep;
And the game killed, or lost, go talk or sleep.

The Will

BEFORE I sigh my last gasp, let me breathe,
Great Love, some legacies; I here bequeath
Mine eyes to Argus, if mine eyes can see;
If they be blind, then, Love, I give them thee;
My tongue to Fame; to ambassadors mine ears;
        To women or the sea, my tears:
    Thou, Love, hast taught me heretofore
By making me serve her who had twenty more,
That I should give to none, but such as had too much before.

My constancy I to the planets give;
My truth to them who at the court do live;
Mine ingenuity and openness,
To Jesuits; to buffoons my pensiveness;
My silence to any, who abroad hath been;
        My money to a Capuchin:
    Thou, Love, taught'st me, by appointing me
To love there, where no love received can be,
Only to give to such as have an incapacity.

My faith I give to Roman Catholics;
All my good works unto the Schismatics
Of Amsterdam; my best civility
And courtship to an University;

My modesty I give to soldiers bare;
My patience let gamesters share:
Thou, Love, taught'st me, by making me
Love her that holds my love disparity,
Only to give to those that count my gifts indignity.

I give my reputation to those
Which were my friends; mine industry to foes;
To schoolmen I bequeath my doubtfulness;
My sickness to physicians, or excess;
To nature all that I in rhyme have writ;
And to my company my wit:
Thou, Love, by making me adore
Her, who begot this love in me before,
Taught'st me to make, as though I gave, when I do but restore.

To him for whom the passing-bell next tolls,
I give my physic books; my written rolls
Of moral counsels I to Bedlam give;
My brazen medals unto them which live
In want of bread; to them which pass among
All foreigners, mine English tongue:
Thou, Love, by making me love one
Who thinks her friendship a fit portión
For younger lovers, dost my gifts thus disproportión.

Therefore I'll give no more, but I'll undo
The world by dying, because love dies too.
Then all your beauties will be no more worth
Than gold in mines, where none doth draw it forth;
And all your graces no more use shall have,
Than a sundial in a grave:

Thou, Love, taught'st me by making me
Love her who doth neglect both me and thee,
To invent, and practise this one way, to annihilate all three.

The Legacy

WHEN I died last, and, dear, I die
  As often as from thee I go,
  Though it be but an hour ago,
And lovers' hours be full eternity,
I can remember yet, that I
  Something did say, and something did bestow;
Though I be dead, which sent me, I should be
Mine own executor and legacy.

  I heard me say, Tell her anon,
    That my self (that is you, not I,)
    Did kill me, and when I felt me die,
  I bid me send my heart, when I was gone;
  But I alas could there fine none,
    When I had ripped me, and searched where
      hearts did lie;
  It killed me again, that I who still was true,
  In life, in my last Will should cozen you.

  Yet I found something like a heart,
    But colors it, and corners had,
    It was not good, it was not bad,
  It was entire to none, and few had part.
  As good as could be made by art
    It seemed; and therefore for our losses sad,
  I meant to send this heart instead of mine,
  But oh, no man could hold it, for 't was thine.

The Prohibition

TAKE heed of loving me,
At least remember, I forbade it thee;
Not that I shall repair my unthrifty waste
Of breath and blood, upon thy sighs, and tears,
By being to thee then what to me thou wast;
But so great joy our life at once outwears,
Then, lest thy love, by my death, frustrate be,
If thou love me, take head of loving me.

Take heed of hating me,
Or too much triumph in the victory.
Not that I shall be mine own officer,
And hate with hate again retaliate;
But thou wilt lose the style of conqueror,
If I, thy conquest, perish by thy hate.
Then, lest my being nothing lessen thee,
If thou hate me, take heed of hating me.

Yet, love and hate me too,
So, these extremes shall neither's office do;
Love me, that I may die the gentler way;
Hate me, because thy love is too great for me;
Or let these two, themselves, not me decay.
So shall I, live, thy stage, not triumph be;
Lest thou thy love and hate and me undo,
To let me live, O love and hate me too.

The Dissolution

SHE'S dead; and all which die
    To their first elements resolve;
And we were mutual elements to us,
    And made of one another.
My body then doth hers involve,
And those things whereof I consist hereby
In me abundant grow, and burdenous,
    And nourish not, but smother.
My fire of passion, sighs of air,
Water of tears, and earthy sad despair,
    Which my materials be.
But near worn out by love's security,
She, to my loss, doth by her death repair.
And I might live long wretched so,
But that my fire doth with my fuel grow.
    Now, as those active kings
  Whose foreign conquest treasure brings,
Receive more, and spend more, and soonest break,
This—which I am amazed that I can speak—
    This death hath with my store
      My use increased.
And so my soul, more earnestly released,
Will outstrip hers; as bullets flown before
A later bullet may o'ertake, the powder being more.

The Damp

WHEN I am dead, and doctors know not why,
        And my friends' curiosity
Will have me cut up to survey each part,
When they shall find your picture in my heart,
        You think a sudden damp of love
        Will through all their senses move,
And work on them as me, and so prefer
Your murder to the name of massacre.

Poor victories; but if you dare be brave,
        And pleasure in your conquest have,
First kill the enormous giant, your Disdain;
And let th' enchantress Honor, next be slain;
        And like a Goth or Vandal rise,
        Deface records and histories
Of your own arts and triumphs over men,
And without such advantage kill me then.

For I could muster up, as well as you,
        My giants, and my witches, too,
Which are vast Constancy and Secretness;
But these I neither look for nor profess;
        Kill me as woman, let me die
        As a mere man; do you but try
Your passive valor, and you shall find then,
Naked you have odds enough of any man.

The Flea

MARK but this flea, and mark in this,
How little that which thou deny'st me is;
It sucked me first, and now sucks thee,
And in this flea, our two bloods mingled be;
Thou know'st that this cannot be said
A sin, nor shame, nor loss of maidenhead,
    Yet this enjoys before it woo,
    And pampered swells with one blood made of two,
    And this, alas, is more than we would do.

Oh stay, three lives in one flea spare,
Where we almost, yea, more than married are.
This flea is you and I, and this
Our marriage bed, and marriage temple is;
Though parents grudge, and you, we're met,
And cloistered in these living walls of jet.
    Though use make you apt to kill me,
    Let not to that, self murder added be,
    And sacrilege, three sins in killing three.

Cruel and sudden, hast thou since
Purpled thy nail, in blood of innocence?
Wherein could this flea guilty be,
Except in that drop which it sucked from thee?
Yet thou triumph'st, and say'st that thou
Find'st not thyself, nor me the weaker now;
    'T is true, then learn how false, fears be;
    Just so much honor, when thou yield'st to me,
    Will waste, as this flea's death took life from thee.

The Bait

COME live with me, and be my love,
And we will some new pleasures prove
Of golden sands, and crystal brooks,
With silken lines and silver hooks.

There will the river whispering run
Warmed by thy eyes, more than the Sun.
And there th' enamored fish will stay,
Begging themselves they may betray.

When thou wilt swim in that live bath,
Each fish, which every channel hath,
Will amorously to thee swim,
Gladder to catch thee, than thou him.

If thou, to be so seen, be'st loth,
By Sun, or Moon, thou dark'nest both,
And if myself have leave to see,
I need not their light, having thee.

Let others freeze with angling reeds,
And cut their legs with shells and weeds,
Or treacherously poor fish beset,
With strangling snare or windowy net:

Let coarse bold hands, from slimy nest
The bedded fish in banks out-wrest,
Or curious traitors, sleeve-silk flies
Bewitch poor fishes' wand'ring eyes.

For thee, thou need'st no such deceit,
For thou thyself art thine own bait;
That fish, that is not catched thereby,
Alas, is wiser far than I.

The Undertaking

I HAVE done one braver thing
    Than all the worthies did;
And yet a braver thence doth spring,
    Which is, to keep that hid.

It were but madness now to impart
    The skill of specular stone,
When he, which can have learned the art
    To cut it, can find none.

So, if I now should utter this,
    Others—because no more
Such stuff to work upon, there is—
    Would love but as before.

But he who loveliness within
    Hath found, all outward loathes,
For he who color loves, and skin,
    Loves but their oldest clothes.

If, as I have, you also do
    Virtue in woman see,
And dare love that, and say so, too,
    And forget the He and She;

And if this love, though placéd so,
   From profane men you hide,
Which will no faith on this bestow,
   Or, if they do, deride;

Then you have done a braver thing
   Than all the worthies did;
And a braver thence will spring,
   Which is, to keep that hid.

The Relic

WHEN my grave is broke up again
Some second guest to entertain,
(For graves have learned that woman-head
   To be to more than one a bed)
     And he that digs it, spies
A bracelet of bright hair about the bone,
     Will he not let us alone,
And think that there a loving couple lies,
Who thought that this device might be some way
To make their souls, at the last busy day,
Meet at this grave, and make a little stay?

   If this fall in a time, or land,
   Where mis-devotion doth command,
   Then, he that digs us up, will bring
   Us, to the Bishop, and the King,
     To make us relics; then
Thou shalt be a Mary Magadalen, and I
     A something else thereby.

All women shall adore us, and some men;
And since at such time, miracles are sought,
I would have that age by this paper taught
What miracles we harmless lovers wrought.

        First, we loved well and faithfully,
        Yet knew not what we loved, nor why,
        Difference of sex no more we knew,
        Than our Guardian Angels do;
           Coming and going, we
Perchance might kiss, but not between those meals;
          Our hands ne'er touched the seals,
Which nature, injured by late law, sets free:
These miracles we did; but now alas,
All measure, and all language, I should pass,
Should I tell what a miracle she was.

The Funeral

WHOEVER comes to shroud me, do not harm
      Nor question much
That subtle wreath of hair, which crowns my arm;
The mystery, the sign you must not touch,
      For 't is my outward soul,
Viceroy to that, which then to heaven being gone,
      Will leave this to control,
And keep these limbs, her provinces, from dissolutión.

For if the sinewy thread my brain lets fall
      Through every part,
Can tie those parts, and make me one of all;
These hairs which upward grew, and strength and art
      Have from a better brain,
Can better do 't; except she meant that I
      By this should know my pain,
As prisoners then are manacled, when they're condemned to
    die.

Whate'er she meant by it, bury it with me,
      For since I am
Love's martyr, it might breed idolatry,
If into others' hands these relics came;
      As 't was humility
To afford to it all that a soul can do,
      So, 't is some bravery,
That since you would save none of me, I bury some of you.

Absence[1]

That time and absence proves
Rather helps than hurts to loves.

ABSENCE, hear thou my protestation
    Against thy strength,
    Distance, and length;
Do what thou canst for alteration,
    For hearts of truest mettle
    Absence doth join and time doth settle.

Who loves a mistress of such quality,
    His mind hath found
    Affection's ground
Beyond time, place, and all mortality;
    To hearts that cannot vary
    Absence is present, Time doth tarry.

My senses want their outward motion,
    Which now within
    Reason doth win,
Redoubled by her secret notion;
    Like rich men that take pleasure
    In hiding more than handling treasure.

By absence this good means I gain,
    That I can catch her,
    Where none can watch her,
In some close corner of my brain;
    There I embrace and kiss her,
    And so enjoy her, and none miss her.

[1] This is one of Donne's "doubtful" poems. However, it appears in the Stephens Manuscript as well as the Harvey Manuscript of Donne and in several other places. Moreover, the manner, as well as the matter, is definitely in Donne's peculiar style.

II

---- * ----

Break of Day: 1

STAY, O sweet, and do not rise;
The light that shines comes from thine eyes;
The day breaks not, it is my heart,
Because that you and I must part.
   Stay, or else my joys will die
   And perish in their infancy.

Break of Day: 2

'T IS true, 't is day; what though it be?
O, wilt thou therefore rise from me?
Why should we rise because 't is light?
Did we lie down because 't was night?
Love, which in spite of darkness brought us hither,
Should in despite of light keep us together.

Light hath no tongue, but is all eye.
If it could speak as well as spy,
This were the worst that it could say,
That being well I fain would stay,
And that I loved my heart and honor so,
That I would not from him that had them go.

Must business thee from hence remove?
O! that's the worst disease of love,
The poor, the foul, the false, love can
Admit, but not the busied man.
He which hath business, and makes love, doth do
Such wrong, as when a married man doth woo.

Confined Love

SOME man unworthy to be possessor
Of old or new love, himself being false or weak,
   Thought his pain and shame would be lesser,
If on womankind he might his anger wreak,
      And thence a law did grow,
      One might but one man know;
      But are other creatures so?

   Are sun, moon, or stars by law forbidden,
To smile where they list, or lend away their light?
   Are birds divorced, or are they chidden
If they leave their mate, or lie abroad a-night?
      Beasts do no jointures lose
      Though they new lovers choose,
      But we are made worse than those.

   Whoe'r rigged fair ships to lie in harbors,
And not to seek new lands, or not to deal with all?
   Or built fair houses, set trees, and arbors,
Only to lock up, or else to let them fall?
      Good is not good, unless
      A thousand it possess,
      But doth waste with greediness.

Love's Usury

FOR every hour that thou wilt spare me now,
      I will allow,
Usurious god of love, twenty to thee,
When with my brown my grey hairs equal be.
Till then, Love, let my body range, and let
Me travel, sojourn, snatch, plot, have, forget,
Resume my last year's relic; think that yet
      We'd never met.

Let me think any rival's mine,
      And at next nine
Keep midnight's promise; mistake by the way
The maid, and tell the lady of that delay;
Only let me love none; no, not the sport
From country grass to confitures of court,
Or city's *quelque chose*. Let not report
      My mind transport.

This bargain's good. If when I'm old, I be
      Inflamed by thee,
If thine own honor, or my shame and pain,
Thou covet most, at that age thou shalt gain.
Do thy will then; then subject and degree
And fruit of love, Love, I submit to thee.
Spare me till then; I'll bear it, though she be
      One that love me.

Love's Growth

I SCARCE believe my love to be so pure
As I had thought it was,
Because it doth endure
Vicissitude, and season, as the grass;
Methinks I lied all winter, when I swore
My love was infinite, if spring make it more.

But if this medicine, love, which cures all sorrow
With more, not only be no quintessence,
But mixed of all stuffs, vexing soul, or sense,
And of the sun his active vigor borrow,
Love's not so pure, and abstract as they use
To say, which have no mistress but their Muse;
But as all else, being elemented too,
Love sometimes would contemplate, sometimes do.

And yet no greater, but more eminent,
Love by the spring is grown;
As in the firmament
Stars by the sun are not enlarged, but shown,
Gentle love deeds, as blossoms on a bough,
From love's awakened root do bud out now.

If, as in water stirred, more circles be
Produced by one, love such additions take,
Those like so many spheres but one heaven make;
For they are all concentric unto thee;
And though each spring do add to love new heat,
As princes do in times of action get
New taxes, and remit them not in peace,
No winter shall abate this spring's increase.

Love's Exchange

LOVE, any devil else but you
Would for a given soul give something too.
At court your fellows every day
Give th' art of rhyming, huntsmanship, or play,
For them which were their own before;
Only I have nothing, which gave more,
But am, alas! by being lowly, lower.

I ask no dispensation now,
To falsify a tear, or sigh, or vow;
I do not sue from thee to draw
A *non obstante* on nature's law;
These are prerogatives, they inhere
In thee and thine; none should forswear
Except that he Love's minion were.

Give me thy weakness, make me blind,
Both ways, as thou and thine, in eyes and mind;
Love, let me never know that this
Is love, or, that love childish is;
Let me not know that others know
That she knows my pains, lest that so
A tender shame make me mine own new woe.

If thou give nothing, yet thou 'rt just,
Because I would not thy first motions trust;
Small towns which stand stiff, till great shot
Enforce them, by war's law condition not;
Such in Love's warfare is my case;
I may not article for grace,
Having put Love at last to show this face.

This face, by which he could command
And change th' idolatry of any land,
This face, which, wheresoe'er it comes,
Can call vowed men from cloisters, dead from tombs,
And melt both poles at once, and store
Deserts with cities, and make more
Mines in the earth, then quarries were before.

For this Love is enraged with me,
Yet kills not; if I must example be
To future rebels, if th' unborn
Must learn by my being cut up and torn,
Kill, and dissect me, Love; for this
Torture against thine own end is.
Racked carcasses make ill anatomies.

Lovers' Infiniteness

IF yet I have not all thy love,
Dear, I shall never have it all;
I cannot breathe one other sigh, to move,
Nor can entreat one other tear to fall;
And all my treasure, which should purchase thee,
Sighs, tears, and oaths, and letters I have spent;
Yet no more can be due to me,
Than at the bargain made was meant.
If then thy gift of love were partiál,
That some to me, some should to others fall,
    Dear, I shall never have thee all.

Or if then thou gavest me all,
All was but all, which thou hadst then;

But if in thy heart since there be or shall
New love created be by other men,
Which have their stocks entire, and can in tears,
In sighs, in oaths, and letters, outbid me,
This new love may beget new fears,
For this love was not vowed by thee.
And yet it was, thy gift being general;
The ground, thy heart, is mine; whatever shall
   Grow there, dear, I should have it all.

Yet I would not have all yet.
He that hath all can have no more;
And since my love doth every day admit
New growth, thou shouldst have new rewards in store.
Thou canst not every day give me thy heart,
If thou canst give it, then thou never gavest it;
Love's riddles are, that though thy heart depart,
It stays at home, and thou with losing savest it;
But we will have a way more liberal,
Than changing hearts, to join them; so we shall
   Be one, and one another's all.

Love's Alchemy

SOME that have deeper digged love's mine than I,
Say, where his centric happiness doth lie:
     I have loved, and got, and told,
But should I love, get, tell, till I were old,
I should not find that hidden mystery.
     Oh! 't is imposture all:
And as no chemic yet th' elixir got,
     But glorifies his pregnant pot,
     If by the way to him befall
Some odoriferous thing, or medicinal,
  So, lovers dream a rich and long delight,
  But get a winter-seeming summer's night.

Our ease, our thrift, our honor, and our day,
Shall we, for this vain bubble's shadow play?
     Ends love in this, that my man,
Can be as happy as I can, if he can
Endure the short scorn of a bridegroom's play?
     That loving wretch that swears,
'T is not the bodies marry, but the minds,
     Which he in her angelic finds,
     Would swear as justly, that he hears,
In that day's rude hoarse minstrelsy, the spheres.
  Hope not for mind in women; at their best
  Sweetness and wit, they are but mummy, possessed.

A Valediction of Weeping

LET me pour forth
My tears before thy face, whilst I stay here,
For thy face coins them, and thy stamp they bear,
And by this mintage they are something worth,
        For thus they be
        Pregnant of thee;
Fruits of much grief they are, emblems of more;
When a tear falls, that thou fall'st which it bore;
So thou and I are nothing then, when on a divers shore.

On a round ball
A workman that hath copies by, can lay
An Europe, Afric, and an Asia,
And quickly make that, which was nothing, All.
        So doth each tear,
        Which thee doth wear,
A globe, yea, world by that impression grow,
Till thy tears mixt with mine do overflow
This world, by waters sent from thee, my heaven dissolvéd
        so.

O! more than Moon,
Draw not up seas to drown me in thy sphere,
Weep me not dead, in thine arms, but forbear
To teach the sea, what it may do too soon;
        Let not the wind
        Example find,
To do me more harm, than it purposeth;
Since thou and I sigh one another's breath,
Whoe'er sighs most, is cruellest, and hastes the other's
        death.

A Valediction Forbidding Mourning

AS virtuous men pass mildly away,
   And whisper to their souls, to go,
Whilst some of their sad friends do say,
   The breath goes now, and some say, no:

So let us melt, and make no noise,
   No tear-floods, nor sigh-tempests move,
'T were profanation of our joys
   To tell the laity our love.

Moving of th' earth brings harms and fears,
   Men reckon what it did and meant,
But trepidation of the spheres,
   Though greater far, is innocent.

Dull sublunary lovers love
   (Whose soul is sense) cannot admit
Absence, because it doth remove
   Those things which elemented it.

But we by a love, so much refined,
   That our selves know not what it is,
Inter-assuréd of the mind,
   Care less, eyes, lips, and hands to miss.

Our two souls therefore, which are one,
   Though I must go, endure not yet
A breach, but an expansión,
   Like gold to airy thinness beat.

If they be two, they are two so
 As stiff twin compasses are two,
Thy soul the fixed foot, makes no show
 To move, but doth, if th' other do.

And though it in the center sit,
 Yet, when the other far doth roam,
It leans, and hearkens after it,
 And grows erect, as that comes home.

Such wilt thou be to me, who must
 Like th' other foot, obliquely run;
Thy firmness draws my circle just,
 And makes me end, where I begun.

A Nocturnal Upon St. Lucy's Day,
Being the Shortest Day

'T IS the year's midnight, and it is the day's, *darkest time of the year.*
Lucy's, who scarce seven hours herself unmasks;
   The sun is spent, and now his flasks
   Send forth light squibs, *brief witty writing* no constant rays;
      The world's whole sap is sunk;
The general balm th' hydroptic earth hath drunk, *Compared to me the depressed world seems joyous*
Whither, as to the bed's-feet, life is shrunk,
Dead and interred; yet all these seem to laugh, *I am lower than low*
Compared with me, who am their epitaph.

Study me then, you who shall lovers be
At the next world, that is, at the next spring;
   For I am a very dead thing,
   In whom Love wrought new alchemy.
      For his art did express *purest essence of something*
A quintessence even from nothingness,
From dull privations, and lean emptiness;
He ruined me, and I am re-begot
Of absence, darkness, death—things which are not.

All others, from all things, draw all that's good,
Life, soul, form, spirit, whence they being have;
   I, by Love's limbec,[1] am the grave
   Of all, that's nothing. Oft a flood
      Have we two wept, and so
Drowned the whole world, us two; oft did we grow,
To be two chaoses, when we did show

[1] Limbec: A corruption of *alembic*, an Arabian word for the jar or vessel in which chemicals were vaporized.

[209]

Care to aught else; and often absences
Withdrew our souls, and made us carcasses.

But I am by her death—which word wrongs her—
Of the first nothing the elixir grown;
   Were I a man, that I were one
   I needs must know; I should prefer,
      If I were any beast,
Some ends, some means; yea plants, yea stones detest,
And love; all, all some properties invest.
If I an ordinary nothing were,
As shadow, a light, and body must be here.

But I am none; nor will my sun renew.
You lovers, for whose sake the lesser sun
   At this time to the Goat is run   Capricorn
   To fetch new lust, and give it you,   Winter
      Enjoy your summer all,
Since she enjoys her long night's festival.
Let me prepare towards her, and let me call
This hour her vigil, and her eve, since this
Both the year's and the day's deep midnight is.

The Curse

WHOEVER guesses, thinks, or dreams, he knows
Who is my mistress, wither by this curse;
      Him, only for his purse,
      May some dull whore to love dispose,
And then yield unto all that are his foes;
   May he be scorned by one, whom all else scorn,
   Forswear to others, what to her he hath sworn,
   With fear of missing, shame of getting, torn.

Madness his sorrow, gout his cramps, may he
Make, by but thinking who hath made them such;
      And may he feel no touch
      Of conscience, but of fame, and be
Anguished, not that 't was sin, but that 't was she;
   Or may he for her virtue reverence
   One that hates him only for impotence,
   And equal traitors be she and his sense.

May he dream treason, and believe that he
Meant to perform it, and confess, and die,
      And no record tell why;
      His sons, which none of his may be,
Inherit nothing but his infamy;
   Or may he so long parasites have fed,
   That he would fain be theirs whom he hath bred,
   And at the last be circumcised for bread.

The venom of all stepdames, gamesters' gall,
What tyrants and their subjects interwish,
      What plants, mine, beasts, fowl, fish,
      Can contribute, all ill, which all
Prophets or poets spake, and all which shall
   Be annexed in schedules unto this by me,
   Fall on that man; for if it be a she
   Nature beforehand hath out-curséd me.

The Message

SEND home my long strayed eyes to me,
Which, O! too long have dwelt on thee;
Yet since there they have learned such ill,
    Such forced fashions,
    And false passions,
        That they be
        Made by thee
Fit for no good sight, keep them still.

Send home my harmless heart again,
Which no unworthy thought could stain;
But if it be taught by thine
    To make jestings
    Of protestings,
        And break both
        Word and oath,
Keep it, for then 't is none of mine.

Yet send me back my heart and eyes,
That I may know, and see thy lies,
And may laugh and joy, when thou
    Art in anguish
    And dost languish
        For some one
        That will none,
Or prove as false as thou art now.

The Broken Heart

HE is stark mad, who ever says,
   That he hath been in love an hour,
Yet not that love so soon decays,
   But that it can ten in less space devour;
Who will believe me, if I swear
That I have had the plague a year?
   Who would not laugh at me, if I should say,
   I saw a flask of powder burn a day?

Ah, what a trifle is a heart,
   If once into love's hands it come!
All other griefs allow a part
   To other griefs, and ask themselves but some;
They come to us, but us Love draws,
He swallows us, and never chaws:
   By him, as by chained shot, whole ranks do die,
   He is the tyrant pike, our hearts the fry.

If 't were not so, what did become
   Of my heart, when I first saw thee!
I brought a heart into the room,
   But from the room, I carried none with me:
If it had gone to thee, I know
Mine would have taught thine heart to show
   More pity unto me: but Love, alas,
   At one first blow did shiver it as glass.

Yet nothing can to nothing fall,
   Nor any place be empty quite,
Therefore I think my breast hath all
   Those pieces still, though they be not unite;

And now as broken glasses show
A hundred lesser faces, so
   My rags of heart can like, wish, and adore,
   But after one such love, can love no more.

The Indifferent

I CAN love both fair and brown;
Her whom abundance melts, and her whom want betrays,
Her who loves loneness best, and her who masks and plays,
Her whom the country formed, and whom the town,
Her who believes, and her who tries,
Her who still weeps with spongy eyes,
And her who is dry cork, and never cries;
I can love her, and her, and you and you,
I can love any, so she be not true.

Will no other vice content you?
Will it not serve your turn to do, as did your mothers?
Or have you all old vices spent, and now would find out
    others?
Or doth a fear, that men are true, torment you?
Oh, we are not, be not you so.
Let me, and do you, twenty know.
Rob me, but bind me not, and let me go.
Must I, who came to travail through you,
Grow your fixed subject, because you are true?

Venus heard me sigh this song,
And by Love's sweetest part, variety, she swore,
She heard not this till now; and that it should be so no more.
She went, examined, and returned ere long,
And said, "Alas, some two or three
Poor heretics in love there be,
Which think to 'stablish dangerous constancy.
But I have told them, 'Since you will be true,
You shall be true to them, who are false to you.' "

The Dream

DEAR love, for nothing less than thee
Would I have broke this happy dream;
      It was a theme
For reason, much too strong for fantasy.
Therefore thou waked'st me wisely; yet
My dream thou brokest not, but continued'st it.
Thou art so true that thoughts of thee suffice
To make dreams truths, and fables histories;
Enter these arms, for since thou thought'st it best,
Not to dream all my dream, let's act the rest.

As lightning, or a taper's light,
Thine eyes, and not thy noise waked me;
      Yet I thought thee
—For thou lovest truth—an angel, at first sight;
But when I saw thou saw'st my heart,
And knew'st my thoughts beyond an angel's art,
When thou knew'st what I dreamt, when thou knew'st when
Excess of joy would wake me, and camest then,
I must confess, it could not choose but be
Profane, to think thee any thing but thee.

Coming and staying showed thee, thee,
But rising makes me doubt, that now
      Thou art not thou.
That love is weak where fear's as strong as he;
'T is not all spirit, pure and brave,
If mixture it of fear, shame, honor have;
Perchance as torches, which must ready be,
Men light and put out, so thou deal'st with me;
Thou camest to kindle, go'st to come; then I
Will dream that hope again, but else would die.

The Apparition

WHEN by thy scorn, O murderess, I am dead,
And that thou think'st thee free
From all solicitation from me,
Then shall my ghost come to thy bed,
And thee, feigned vestal, in worse arms shall see;
Then thy sick taper will begin to wink,
And he, whose thou art then, being tired before,
Will, if thou stir, or pinch to wake him, think
  Thou call'st for more,
And, in false sleep, will from thee shrink:
And then, poor aspen wretch, neglected thou
Bathed in a cold quicksilver sweat will lie
  A verier ghost than I.
What I will say, I will not tell thee now,
Lest that preserve thee; and since my love is spent,
I'd rather thou shouldst painfully repent,
Than by my threatenings rest still innocent.

The Primrose

BEING AT MONTGOMERY CASTLE UPON THE HILL,
ON WHICH IT IS SITUATE

UPON this Primrose Hill,
  Where, if heaven would distill
A shower of rain, each several drop might go
To his own primrose, and grow manna so;
And where their form, and their infinity
  Make a terrestrial galaxy,
  As the small stars do in the sky;

I walk to find a true love; and I see
That 't is not a mere woman, that is she,
But must or more or less than woman be.

Yet know I not, which flower
I wish; a six, or four; [1]
For should my true-love less than woman be,
She were scarce anything; and then, should she
Be more than woman, she would get above
All thought of sex, and think to move
My heart to study her, and not to love.
Both these were monsters; since there must reside
Falsehood in woman, I could more abide,
She were by art, than nature falsified.

Live, primrose, then, and thrive
With thy true number five;
And, woman, whom this flower doth represent,
With this mysterious number be content;
Ten is the farthest number; if half ten
Belongs unto each woman, then
Each woman may take half us men;
Or—if this will not serve their turn—since all
Numbers are odd, or even, and they fall
First into five, women may take us all.

[1] The corolla of the primrose usually consists of five segments. Sometimes, however, primroses are found in which the corolla is divided into four or six parts.

The Blossom

LITTLE think'st thou, poor flower,
  Whom I've watched six or seven days
And seen thy birth, and seen what every hour
Gave to thy growth, thee to this height to raise,
And now dost laugh and triumph on this bough,
      Little think'st thou,
That it will freeze anon, and that I shall
Tomorrow find thee fallen, or not at all.

  Little think'st thou, poor heart,
    That laborest yet to nestle thee,
And think'st by hovering here to get a part
In a forbidden or forbidding tree,
And hopest her stiffness by long siege to bow,
      Little think'st thou,
That thou tomorrow, ere that sun doth wake,
Must with this sun and me a journey take.

  But thou which lovest to be
    Subtle to plague thyself, wilt say,
"Alas! if you must go, what's that to me?
Here lies my business, and here I will stay;
You go to friends, whose love and means present
      Various content
To your eyes, ears, and taste, and every part;
If then your body go, what need your heart?"

  Well, then, stay here; but know,
    When thou hast stayed and done thy most,
A naked thinking heart that makes no show,
Is to a woman but a kind of ghost.

How shall she know my heart; or having none,
        Know thee for one?
Practice may make her know some other part;
But take my word, she doth not know a heart.

  Meet me at London, then,
   Twenty days hence, and thou shalt see
Me fresher, and more fat, by being with men,
Than if I had stayed still with her and thee.
For God's sake, if you can, be you so, too.
       I will give you
There to another friend, whom we shall find
As glad to have my body as my mind.

III

Woman's Constancy

NOW thou hast loved me one whole day,
Tomorrow when thou leav'st, what wilt thou say?
Wilt thou then antedate some new-made vow?
      Or say that now
We are not just those persons, which we were?
Or that oaths made in reverential fear
Of Love, and his wrath, any may forswear?
Or, as true deaths true marriages untie,
So lovers' contracts, images of those,
Bind but till sleep, death's image, them unloose?
      Or, your own end to justify,
For having purposed change, and falsehood, you
Can have no way but falsehood to be true?
Vain lunatic, against these 'scapes I could
      Dispute, and conquer, if I would,
      Which I abstain to do;
For by tomorrow, I may think so too.

Community

GOOD we must love, and must hate ill,
For ill is ill, and good good still,
  But there are things indifferent,
Which we may neither hate nor love,
But one, and then another prove,
  As we shall find our fancy bent.

If then at first wise Nature had
Made women either good or bad,
  Then some we might hate, and some choose;
But since she did them so create,
That we may neither love nor hate,
  Only this rests, all all may use.

If they were good it would be seen,
Good is as visible as green,
  And to all eyes itself betrays:
If they were bad, they could not last,
Bad doth itself, and others waste,
  So they deserve nor blame, nor praise.

But they are ours as fruits are ours,
He that but tastes, he that devours,
  And he that leaves all, doth as well:
Changed loves are but changed sorts of meat,
And when he hath the kernel eat,
  Who doth not fling away the shell?

Witchcraft by a Picture

I FIX mine eye on thine, and there
    Pity my picture burning in thine eye;
My picture drowned in a transparent tear,
    When I look lower I espy;
      Hadst thou the wicked skill
By pictures made and marred, to kill,
How many ways might'st thou perform thy will?

But now I've drunk thy sweet salt tears,
    And though thou pour more, I'll depart;
My picture vanished, vanish all fears
    That I çan be endamaged by that art;
      Though thou retain of me
One picture more, yet that will be,
Being in thine own heart, from all malice free.

His Picture

HERE take my picture; though I bid farewell,
Thine, in my heart, where my soul dwells, shall dwell.
'T is like me now, but I dead 't will be more,
When we are shadows both, than 't was before.
When weatherbeaten I come back; my hand
Perhaps with rude oars torn, or sunbeams tanned,
My face and breast of haircloth, and my head
With care's harsh sudden hoariness o'erspread,
My body a sack of bones, broken within,
And powder's blue stains scattered on my skin;
If rival fools tax thee to have loved a man,
So foul and coarse, as, O! I may seem then,
This shall say what I was; and thou shalt say,
"Do his hurts reach me? doth my worth decay?
Or do they reach his judging mind, that he
Should now love less, what he did love to see?
That which in him was fair and delicate,
Was but the milk, which in love's childish state
Did nurse it; who now is grown strong enough
To feed on that, which to weak tastes seems tough."

A Fever

O! DO not die, for I shall hate
   All women so, when thou art gone,
That thee I shall not celebrate,
   When I remember, thou wast one.

But yet thou canst not die, I know,
   To leave this world behind, is death,
But when thou from this world wilt go,
   The whole world vapors with thy breath.

Or if, when thou, the world's soul, goest,
   It stay, 't is but thy carcass then,
The fairest woman, but thy ghost,
   But corrupt worms, the worthiest men.

O wrangling schools, that search what fire
   Shall burn this world, had none the wit
Unto this knowledge to aspire,
   That this her fever might be it?

And yet she cannot waste by this,
   Nor long bear this torturing wrong,
For such corruption needful is
   To fuel such a fever long.

These burning fits but meteors be,
   Whose matter in thee is soon spent.
Thy beauty, and all parts, which are thee,
   Are unchangeable firmament.

Yet 't was of my mind, seizing thee,
   Though it in thee cannot persever.
For I had rather owner be
   Of thee one hour, than all else ever.

Air and Angels

TWICE or thrice had I loved thee,
Before I knew thy face or name;
So in a voice, so in a shapeless flame,
Angels affect us oft, and worshipped be;
   Still when, to where thou wert, I came,
Some lovely glorious nothing I did see.
   But since my soul, whose child love is,
Takes limbs of flesh, and else could nothing do,
   More subtle than the parent is,
Love must not be, but take a body too,
    And therefore what thou wert, and who,
      I bid love ask, and now
That it assume thy body, I allow,
And fix itself in thy lip, eye, and brow.

Whilst thus to ballast love, I thought,
And so more steadily to have gone,
With wares which would sink admiration,
I saw, I had love's pinnace overfraught,
   Thy every hair for love to work upon
Is much too much; some fitter must be sought;
   For, nor in nothing, nor in things
Extreme, and scattering bright, can love inhere;
   Then as an Angel, face, and wings
Of air, not pure as it, yet pure doth wear,
    So thy love may be my love's sphere;
      Just such disparity
As is 'twixt air's and angel's purity,
'Twixt women's love, and men's will ever be.

Twickenham Garden

BLASTED with sighs, and surrounded with tears,
    Hither I come to seek the spring,
    And at mine eyes, and at mine ears,
Receive such balms, as else cure everything;
    But O, self-traitor, I do bring
The spider Love, which transubstantiates all,
    And can convert manna to gall,
And that this place may thoroughly be thought
    True paradise, I have the serpent brought.

'T were wholesomer for me, that winter did
    Benight the glory of this place,
    And that a grave frost did forbid
These trees to laugh, and mock me to my face;
    But that I may not this disgrace
Endure, nor yet leave loving, Love, let me
    Some senseless piece of this place be;
Make me a mandrake, so I may groan here,
    Or a stone fountain weeping out my year.

Hither with crystal vials, lovers come,
    And take my tears, which are love's wine,
    And try your mistress' tears at home,
For all are false, that taste not just like mine;
    Alas, hearts do not in eyes shine,
Nor can you more judge woman's thoughts by tears,
    Than by her shadow, what she wears.
O perverse sex, where none is true but she,
    Who's therefore true, because her truth kills me.

The Triple Fool

I AM two fools, I know,
  For loving, and for saying so
    In whining poetry;
But where's that wise man, that would not be I,
    If she would not deny?
Then as th' earth's inward narrow crooked lanes
  Do purge sea water's fretful salt away,
I thought, if I could draw my pains
  Through rhyme's vexation, I should them allay.
Grief brought to numbers cannot be so fierce,
For he tames it, that fetters it in verse.

But when I have done so,
  Some man, his art and voice to show,
    Doth set and sing my pain;
And, by delighting many, frees again
    Grief, which verse did restrain.
To love and grief tribute of verse belongs,
  But not of such as pleases when 't is read.
Both are increased by such songs,
  For both their triumphs so are publishéd,
And I, which was two fools, do so grow three.
Who are a little wise, the best fools be.

A Jet Ring Sent

THOU are not so black, as my heart,
Nor half so brittle, as her heart, thou art;
What would'st thou say? Shall both our properties by thee
be spoke?
Nothing more endless, nothing sooner broke?

Marriage rings are not of this stuff;
O, why should ought less precious, or less tough
Figure our loves? Except in thy name thou have bid it say,
"I am cheap, and nought but fashion, fling me away."

Yet stay with me since thou art come,
Circle this finger's top, which did'st her thumb; [1]
Be justly proud, and gladly safe, that thou dost dwell with
me;
She that, O! broke her faith, would soon break thee.

[1] Thumb-rings were often worn in the seventeenth century. Shakespeare's Falstaff claimed that he was once so slender he could have slipped through an alderman's thumb-ring.

Negative Love

I NEVER stooped so low, as they
Which on an eye, cheek, lip, can prey,
   Seldom to them, which soar no higher
   Than virtue or the mind to admire,
For sense, and understanding may
   Know, what gives fuel to their fire:
My love, though silly, is more brave,
For may I miss, whene'er I crave,
If I know yet what I would have.

If that be simply perfectest
Which can by no way be expressed
   But Negatives, my love is so.
   To all, which all love, I say no.
If any who deciphers best,
   What we know not — our selves — can know,
Let him teach me that nothing. This
As yet my ease, and comfort is,
Though I speed not, I cannot miss.

The Expiration

SO, so, break off this last lamenting kiss,
  Which sucks two souls, and vapors both away;
Turn thou ghost that way, and let me turn this,
  And let ourselves benight our happiest day,
We asked none leave to love; nor will we owe
  Any so cheap a death, as saying, "Go."

Go; and if that word have not quite killed thee,
  Ease me with death, by bidding me go too.
O, if it have, let my word work on me,
  And a just office on a murderer do.
Except it be too late, to kill me so,
  Being double dead, going, and bidding, "Go."

The Computation

FOR my first twenty years, since yesterday,
  I scarce believed thou could'st be gone away,
For forty more I fed on favors past,
  And forty on hopes, that thou would'st they might last.
Tears drowned one hundred, and sighs blew out two,
  A thousand, I did neither think, nor do,
  Or not divide, all being one thought of you;
  Or in a thousand more, forgot that too.
Yet call not this long life; but think that I
Am, by being dead, immortal. Can ghosts die?

The Paradox

NO lover saith, I love, nor any other
    Can judge a perfect lover;
He thinks that else none can, nor will agree
    That any loves but he.
I cannot say I loved, for who can say
    He was killed yesterday?
Love with excess of heat, more young than old,
    Death kills with too much cold;
We die but once, and who loved last did die,
    He that saith, twice, doth lie:
For though he seem to move, and stir a while,
    It doth the sense beguile.
Such life is like the light which bideth yet
    When the life's light is set,
Or like the heat, which fire is solid matter
    Leaves behind, two hours after.
Once I loved and died; and am now become
    Mine epitaph and tomb.
Here dead men speak their last, and so do I;
    Love-slain, lo! here I lie.

Farewell to Love

WHILST yet to prove,
I thought there was some deity in love
So did I reverence, and gave
Worship; as atheists at their dying hour
Call, what they cannot name, an unknown power,
As ignorantly did I crave:
Thus when
Things not yet known are coveted by men,
Our desires give them fashion, and so
As they wax lesser, fall, as they size, grow.

But, from late fair,
His highness sitting in a golden chair,
Is not less cared for after three days
By children, than the thing which lovers so
Blindly admire, and with such worship woo;
Being had, enjoying it decays:
And thence,
What before pleased them all, takes but one sense,
And that so lamely, as it leaves behind
A kind of sorrowing dullness to the mind.

Ah, cannot we,
As well as cocks and lions jocund be,
After such pleasures? Unless wise
Nature decreed (since each such act, they say,
Diminisheth the length of life a day)
This; as she would man should despise
The sport,
Because that other curse of being short,
And only for a minute made to be
Eager desire, to raise posterity.

Since so, my mind
Shall not desire what no man else can find,
    I'll no more dote and run
To pursue things which had endamaged me.
And when I come where moving beauties be.
    As men do when the summer's sun
            Grows great,
Though I admire their greatness, shun their heat;
    Each place can afford shadows. If all fail,
'T is but applying worm-seed to the tail.

A Lecture Upon the Shadow

STAND still, and I will read to thee
A lecture, love, in Love's philosophy.
    These three hours that we have spent,
    Walking here, two shadows went
Along with us, which we ourselves produced;
But, now the sun is just above our head,
    We do those shadows tread;
    And to brave clearness all things are reduced.
    So whilst our infant loves did grow,
    Disguises did, and shadows, flow,
    From us, and our cares; but, now 't is not so.

That love hath not attained the highest degree,
Which is still diligent lest others see.

Except our loves at this noon stay,
We shall new shadows make the other way.
    As the first were made to blind
    Others, these which come behind
Will work upon ourselves, and blind our eyes.
If our loves faint, and westwardly decline;
    To me thou, falsely, thine,
    And I to thee mine actions shall disguise.
    The morning shadows wear away,
    But these grow longer all the day,
    But O! love's day is short, if love decay.

Love is a growing, or full constant light;
And his first minute, after noon, is night.

The Token

SEND me some token, that my hope may live,
  Or that my easeless thoughts may sleep and rest;
Send me some honey to make sweet my hive,
  That in my passion I may hope the best.
I beg no ribbon wrought with thine own hands,
  To knit our loves in the fantastic strain
Of new-touched youth; nor ring to show the stands
  Of our affection, that, as that's round and plain,
So should our loves meet in simplicity.
  No, nor the corals which thy wrist enfold,
Laced up together in congruity,
  To show our thoughts should rest in the same hold;
No, nor thy picture, though most gracious,
  And most desired, because 't is like the best;
Nor witty lines, which are most copious,
  Within the writings which thou hast addressed.

Send me nor this, nor that, to increase my store,
But swear thou think'st I love thee, and no more.

Self-Love

HE that cannot choose but love,
And strives against it still,
Never shall my fancy move;
For he loves against his will;
Nor he which is all his own,
And cannot pleasure choose,
When I am caught he can be gone,
And when he list refuse.
Nor he that loves none but fair,
For such by all are sought;
Nor he that can for foul ones care,
For his judgment then is nought:
Nor he that hath wit, for he
Will make me his jest or slave;
Nor a fool, for when others . . .
He can neither . . .
Nor he that still his mistress pays,
For she is thralled therefore:
Nor he that pays not, for he says
Within, she's worth no more.
Is there then no kind of men
Whom I may freely prove?
I will vent that humor then
In mine own self-love.

IV

———— * ————

Elegy VII: Nature's Lay Idiot

NATURE'S lay idiot, I taught thee to love,
And in that sophistry, O! thou dost prove
Too subtle; fool, thou didst not understand
The mystic language of the eye nor hand;
Nor couldst thou judge the difference of the air
Of sighs, and say, "This lies, this sounds despair";
Nor by th' eye's water cast a malady
Desperately hot, or changing feverously.
I had not taught thee then the alphabet
Of flowers, how they, devisefully being set
And bound up, might with speechless secrecy
Deliver errands mutely, and mutually.
Remember since all thy words used to be
To every suitor, "Ay, if my friends agree";
Since household charms, thy husband's name to teach,
Were all the love-tricks that thy wit could reach;
And since an hour's discourse could scarce have made
One answer in thee, and that ill arrayed
In broken proverbs, and torn sentences,
Thou art not by so many duties his—
That from th' world's common having severed thee,
Inlaid thee, neither to be seen, nor see—
As mine, who have with amorous delicacies
Refined thee into a blissful paradise.
Thy graces and good works my creatures be;
I planted knowledge and life's tree in thee;
Which O! shall strangers taste? Must I, alas!

Frame and enamel plate, and drink in glass?
Chafe wax for other's seals? break a colt's force,
And leave him then, being made a ready horse?

Elegy X: The Dream

IMAGE of her whom I love, more than she,
    Whose fair impression in my faithful heart
Makes me her medal, and makes her love me,
    As kings do coins, to which their stamps impart
The value; go, and take my heart from hence,
    Which now is grown too great and good for me.
Honors oppress weak spirits, and our sense
    Strong objects dull; the more, the less we see.
When you are gone, and reason gone with you,
    Then fantasy is queen and soul, and all;
She can present joys meaner than you do,
    Convenient, and more proportional.
So, if I dream I have you, I have you,
    For all our joys are but fantastical;
And so I 'scape the pain, for pain is true;
    And sleep, which locks up sense, doth lock out all.
After a such fruition I shall wake,
    And, but the waking, nothing shall repent;
And shall to love more thankful sonnets make,
    Than if more honor, tears and pains were spent.
But dearest heart and dearer image, stay;
    Alas! true joys at best are dream enough;
Though you stay here, you pass too fast away,
    For even at first life's taper is a snuff.
Filled with her love, may I be rather grown
    Mad with much heart, than idiot with none.

Elegy XII: His Parting From Her

SINCE she must go, and I must mourn, come night,
Environ me with darkness, whilst I write:
Shadow that hell unto me, which alone
I am to suffer when my love is gone.
Alas! the darkest magic cannot do it,
Thou and great hell to boot are shadows to it.
Should Cynthia quit thee, Venus, and each star,
It would not form one thought dark as mine are.
I could lend thee obscureness now, and say,
Out of myself, there should be no more day,
Such is already my felt want of sight,
Did not the fires within me force a light.
Oh Love, that fire and darkness should be mixed,
Or to thy triumphs so strange torments fixed!
Is it because thou thyself art blind, that we,
Thy martyrs, must no more each other see?
Or tak'st thou pride to break us on the wheel,
And view old Chaos in the pains we feel?
Or have we left undone some mutual rite,
Through holy fear, that merits thy despite?
No, no. The fault was mine, impute it to me,
Or rather to conspiring destiny,
Which (since I loved in jest before) decreed,
That I should suffer when I loved indeed:
And therefore now, sooner than I can say,
I saw the golden fruit, 't is rapt away.
Or as I had watched one drop in a vast stream,
And I left wealthy only in a dream.
Yet Love, thou 'rt blinder than thyself in this,
To vex my dove-like friend for my amiss:
And, where my own sad truth may expiate

Thy wrath, to make her fortune run my fate:
So blinded Justice doth, when favorites fall,
Strike them, their house, their friends, their followers all.
Was 't not enough that thou didst dart thy fires
Into our bloods, inflaming our desires,
And made'st us sigh and glow, and pant, and burn,
And then thyself into our flame did'st turn?
Was 't not enough that thou didst hazard us
To paths in love so dark, so dangerous:
And those so ambushed round with household spies,
And over all, thy husband's towering eyes
That flamed with oily sweat of jealousy:
Yet went we not still on with Constancy?
Have we not kept our guards, like spy on spy?
Had correspondence whilst the foe stood by?
Stolen (more to sweeten them) our many blisses
Of meetings, conference, embracements, kisses?
Shadowed with negligence our most respects?
Varied our language through all dialects,
Of becks, winks, looks, and often under boards
Spoke dialogues with our feet far from our words?
Have we proved all these secrets of our art,
Yea, thy pale inwards, and thy panting heart?
And, after all this passed Purgatory,
Must sad divorce make us the vulgar story?
First let our eyes be riveted quite through
Our turning brains, and both our lips grow to:
Let our arms clasp like ivy, and our fear
Freeze us together, that we may stick here,
Till Fortune, that would rive us, with the deed,
Strain her eyes open, and it make them bleed.
For Love it cannot be, whom hitherto
I have accused, should such a mischief do.

O Fortune, thou'rt not worth my least exclaim,
And plague enough thou hast in thy own shame.
Do thy great worst; my friend and I have arms,
Though not against thy strokes, against thy harms.
Rend us in sunder, thou canst not divide
Our bodies so, but that our souls are tied,
And we can love by letters still and gifts,
And thoughts and dreams. Love never wanteth shifts.
I will not look upon the quickening sun,
But straight her beauty to my sense shall run;
The air shall note her soft, the fire most pure;
Water suggest her clear, and the earth sure.
Time shall not lose our passages; the spring
How fresh our love was in the beginning;
The summer how it ripened in the ear;
And autumn, what our golden harvests were.
The winter I'll not think on to spite thee,
But count it a lost season, so shall she.
And, dearest friend, since we must part, drown night
With hope of day, burdens well born are light.
Though cold and darkness longer hang somewhere,
Yet Phoebus equally lights all the sphere;
And what he cannot in like portions pay,
The world enjoys in mass, and so we may.
Be then ever yourself, and let no woe
Win on your health, your youth, your beauty; so
Declare yourself base Fortune's enemy,
No less by your contempt than constancy:
That I may grow enamored on your mind,
When my own thoughts I there reflected find.
For this to the comfort of my dear I vow,
My deeds shall still be what my words are now;
The poles shall move to teach me ere I start;

And when I change my love, I'll change my heart;
Nay, if I wax but cold in my desire,
Think, heaven hath motion lost, and the world, fire.
Much more I could, but many words have made
That, oft, suspected which men would persuade.
Take therefore all in this: I love so true,
As I will never look for less in you.

Elegy XVII: Elegy On His Mistress

BY our first strange and fatal interview,
By all desires, which thereof did ensue,
By our long starving hopes, by that remorse,
Which my words' masculine persuasive force
Begot in thee, and by the memory
Of hurts, which spies and rivals threatened me,
I calmly beg. But by thy father's wrath,
By all pains, which want and divorcement hath,
I conjure thee; and all the oaths, which I
And thou have sworn to seal joint constancy,
Hear I unswear, and overswear them thus;
Thou shalt not love by ways so dangerous.
Temper, O fair love, Love's impetuous rage,
Be my true mistress still, not my feigned page;
I'll go, and, by thy kind leave, leave behind
Thee, only worthy to nurse in my mind
Thirst to come back. O, if thou die before
My soul from other lands to thee shall soar,
Thy (else almighty) beauty cannot move
Rage from the seas, nor thy love teach them love
Nor tame wild Boreas' harshness; thou hast read
How roughly he in pieces shivered
Fair Orithyia, whom he swore he loved.

Fall ill or good, 't is madness to have proved
Dangers unurged: feed on this flattery,
That absent lovers one in the other be.
Dissemble nothing, not a boy, nor change
Thy body's habit, nor mind; be not strange
To thyself only, all will spy in thy face
A blushing, womanly, discovering grace.
Richly clothed apes are called apes; and as soon
Eclipsed, as bright, we call the moon the moon.
Men of France, changeable chameleons,
Spittles of diseases, shops of fashions,
Love's fuellers, and the rightest company
Of players which upon the world's stage be,
Will quickly know thee; and no less alas,
The indifferent Italian, as we pass
His warm land, well content to think thee page,
Will hunt thee with such lust, and hideous rage,
As Lot's fair guests were vext. But none of these,
Nor spongy hydroptic Dutch, shall thee displease,
If thou stay here. O stay here; for, for thee
England is only a worthy gallery,
To walk in expectation, till from thence
Our greatest king call thee to his presence.
When I am gone, dream me some happiness,
Nor let thy looks our long-hid love confess;
Nor praise, nor dispraise me; nor bless, nor curse
Openly love's force; nor in bed fright thy nurse
With midnight's startings, crying out, O! O!
Nurse, O! my love is slain; I saw him go
O'er the white Alps alone; I saw him, I,
Assailed, taken, fight, stabbed, bleed, fall, and die.
Augur me better chance, except dread Jove
Think it enough for me to have had thy love.

Elegy XX: To His Mistress Going To Bed

COME, madam, come, all rest my powers defy;
Until I labor, I in labor lie.
The foe ofttimes, having the foe in sight,
Is tired with standing, though he never fight.
Off with that girdle, like heaven's zone glittering,
But a far fairer world encompassing.
Unpin that spangled breast-plate, which you wear,
That th' eyes of busy fools may be stopped there.
Unlace yourself, for that harmonious chime
Tells me from you that now it is bedtime.
Off with that happy busk, which I envy,
That still can be, and still can stand so nigh.
Your gown going off such beauteous state reveals,
As when from flowery meads th' hill's shadow steals.
Off with your wiry coronet, and show
The hairy diadems which on you do grow.
Off with your hose and shoes; then softly tread
In this love's hallowed temple, this soft bed.
In such white robes heaven's angels used to be
Revealed to men; thou, angel, bring'st with thee
A heaven-like Mahomet's paradise; and though
Ill spirits walk in white, we easily know
By this these angels from an evil sprite:
Those set our hairs, but these our flesh upright.
Licence my roving hands, and let them go
Before, behind, between, above, and below.
O, my America, my Newfoundland,
My kingdom, safest when with one man manned,
My mine of precious stones, my empery;
How am I blest in thus discovering thee!
To enter in these bonds, is to be free;

Then, where my hand is set, my soul shall be.
Full nakedness! All joys are due to thee;
As souls unbodied, bodies unclothed must be
To taste whole joys. Gems which you women use
Are like Atlanta's ball cast in men's views;
That, when a fool's eye lighteth on a gem,
His earthly soul might court that, not them.
Like pictures, or like books' gay coverings made
For laymen, are all women thus arrayed.
Themselves are only mystic books, which we
—Whom their imputed grace will dignify—
Must see revealed. Then, since that I may know,
As liberally as to thy midwife show
Thyself, cast all, yea, this white linen hence;
There is no penance due to innocence.
To teach thee, I am naked first; why then,
What needst thou have more covering than a man?

To Mrs. Magdalen Herbert

MAD paper, stay, and grudge not here to burn
    With all those sons whom my brain did create;
At least lie hid with me, till thou return
    To rags again, which is thy native state.

What though thou have enough unworthiness
    To come unto great place as others do;
That's much—emboldens, pulls, thrusts, I confess;
    But 't is not all; thou shouldst be wicked, too.

And that thou canst not learn, or not of me,
    Yet thou wilt go; go, since thou goest to her,

Who lacks but faults to be a prince, for she
   Truth, whom they dare not pardon, dares prefer.

But when thou comest to that perplexing eye,
   Which equally claims love and reverence,
Thou wilt not long dispute it, thou wilt die;
   And, having little now, have then no sense.

Yet when her warm redeeming hand — which is
   A miracle, and made such to work more —
Doth touch thee, sapless leaf, thou grow'st by this
   Her creature, glorified more than before.

Then as a mother which delights to hear
   Her early child misspeak half-uttered words,
Or because majesty doth never fear
   Ill or bold speech, she audience affords.

And then, cold speechless wretch, thou diest again,
   And wisely; what discourse is left for thee?
From speech of ill, and her, thou must abstain.
   And is there any good which is not she?

Yet may'st thou praise her servants, though not her;
   And wit, and virtue, and honor her attend;
And since they're but her clothes, thou shalt not err,
   If thou her shape, and beauty, and grace commend.

Who knows thy destiny? When thou hast done,
   Perchance her cabinet may harbor thee,
Whither all noble ambitious wits do run,
   A nest almost as full of good as she.

When thou art there, if any, whom we know,
  Were saved before, and did that heaven partake;
When she revolves his papers, mark what show
  Of favor, she, alone, to them doth make.

Mark if, to get them, she o'erskip the rest;
  Mark if she read them twice, or kiss the name;
Mark if she do the same that thy protest;
  Mark if she mark whether her woman came.

Mark if slight things be objected, and o'erblown;
  Mark if her oaths against him be not still
Reserved, and that she grieves she's not her own,
  And chides the doctrine that denies freewill.

I bid thee not do this to be my spy,
  Nor to make myself her familiar;
But so much I do love her choice, that I
  Would fain love him that shall be loved of her.

Valediction To His Book

I'LL tell thee now, dear love, what thou shalt do
  To anger destiny, as she doth us;
  How I shall stay, though she eloign [1] me thus,
And how posterity shall know it, too;
        How thine may out-endure
        Sibyl's glory, and obscure
        Her who from Pindar could allure,

[1] Banish: From the French *éloigner*.

And her, through whose help Lucan is not lame,
And her, whose book (they say) Homer did find, and name.

Study our manuscripts, those myriads
  Of letters, which have passed 'twixt thee and me;
  Then write our annals, and in them will be
To all whom love's subliming fire invades
        Rule and example found;
        There the faith of any ground
        No schismatic will dare to wound
That sees, how Love this grace to us affords,
To make, to keep, to use, to be these his records.

This book, as long-lived as the elements,
  Or as the world's form, this all-gravéd tome
  In cypher writ, or new made idiom;
We for Love's clergy only are instruments;
        When this book is made thus,
        Should again the ravenous
        Vandals and the Goths invade us,
Learning were safe; in this our universe,
Schools might learn sciences, spheres music, angels verse.

Here Love's divines—since all divinity
  Is love or wonder—may find all they seek,
  Whether abstract spiritual love they like,
Their souls exhaled with what they do not see;
        Or, loth so to amuse
        Faith's infirmity, they choose
        Something which they may see and use;
For, though mind be the heaven, where love doth sit,
Beauty a convenient type may be to figure it.

Here more than in their books may lawyers find,
  Both by what titles mistresses are ours,
  And how prerogative these states devours,
Transferred from Love himself, to womankind;
      Who, though from heart and eyes,
      They exact great subsidies,
      Forsake him who on them relies;
And for the cause, honor, or conscience give;
Chimeras vain as they or their prerogative.

Here statesmen—or of them, they which can read—
  May of their occupation find the grounds;
  Love, and their art, alike it deadly wounds,
If to consider what 't is, one proceed.
      In both they do excel,
      Who the present govern well,
      Whose weakness none doth, or dares tell;
In this thy book, such will there something see,
As in the Bible some can find out alchemy.

Thus vent thy thoughts; abroad I'll study thee,
  As he removes far off, that great heights takes;
  How great love is, presence best trial makes,
But absence tries how long this love will be;
      To take a latitude
      Sun, or stars, are fitliest viewed
      At their brightest, but to conclude
Of longitudes, what other way have we,
But to mark when and where the dark eclipses be?

From "Divine Poems"

BATTER my heart, three-personed God, for you
As yet but knock, breathe, shine, and seek to mend.
That I may rise and stand, o'erthrow me, and bend
Your force, to break, blow, burn, and make me new.
I, like a usurpt town to another due,
Labor to admit you, but O, to no end;
Reason, your victory in me, me should defend,
But is captived, and proves weak or untrue;
Yet dearly I love you, and would be loved fain,
But am betrothed unto your enemy:
Divorce me, untie, or break that knot again,
Take me to you, imprison me, for I,
Except you enthral me, never shall be free;
Nor ever chaste, except you ravish me.